The Only Book You'll Ever Need On Small Business Taxes

Tax Secrets, Legal Loopholes & Deductions to Save You Money

(Plus, Bookkeeping and Accounting for Beginners)

GARRETT MONROE

Contents

Small Business Taxes Done Right

"In this world, nothing is certain except death and taxes."
— **Benjamin Franklin**

The timeless words of Benjamin Franklin still hold true today: taxes are an inevitable reality. For many small business owners, this reality often comes as a harsh surprise. While taxes are an integral part of business operations, managing them effectively can be a daunting challenge.

Consider Sarah, a passionate small business owner who poured her heart and soul into her startup, investing all her resources. She was driven by a dream and focused on growing her business, but she overlooked the critical importance of tax planning. As tax season approached, she was overwhelmed by complex tax deductions, credits, and varying tax rates.. A single missed payment led to costly penalties, and before she knew it, her once-thriving business was in trouble.

Sarah's story is all too common in the small business world. But it doesn't have to be. This book has been crafted to help you overcome such challenges, so you can avoid the pitfalls of growing a business and focus on achieving your entrepreneurial dreams.

The Big Picture: Why This Book Matters

Managing small business taxes can be a challenge. The core objective of this book is simple: to equip small business owners with the knowledge and tools required to steer the often complex and confusing world of taxes. Whether you're just starting or have been in business for years, understanding your tax obligations, maximizing your deductions, and minimizing your liabilities will help you achieve long-term success.

This book will guide you through the intricacies of small business taxes by breaking complicated concepts into practical, actionable steps. By the end, you'll have a solid grasp of tax basics and be equipped with advanced strategies to reduce your tax burden legally. Our goal is to make taxes manageable and help you keep more of what you earn, so you can focus on what you do best: running and growing your business.

What's in It for You: Unlocking the Benefits

This book was written with a clear mission: to provide small business owners with a comprehensive, accessible guide to understanding and managing their taxes effectively. By simplifying these concepts and offering practical advice, this book aims to turn what can often feel like a burden into an opportunity for growth and savings.

One of the key benefits for readers is the potential to save significant amounts of money through well-informed tax planning. This book explores the various deductions available to small business owners, from everyday operational expenses to less obvious tax-saving opportunities. By understanding and applying these deductions, readers can reduce their taxable income and retain more of their hard-earned money.

Beyond deductions, this book examines legal loopholes and strategies to further minimize tax liabilities. These approaches aren't about cutting corners or engaging in risky practices; rather, they focus on making the most out of the legal tools available to every small business owner.

Accurate and detailed financial records are the foundation of any successful tax strategy. This book offers readers practical guidance on maintaining these records accurately, ensuring they are prepared for tax season, as well as any financial challenge that may arise. Proper bookkeeping and accounting are essential for making informed business decisions, and this book provides a solid foundation in these areas.

The content of this book is structured as a step-by-step guide, walking readers through every aspect of small business taxes with clear explanations, real-life examples, and actionable tips. Whether you are filing your taxes for the first time or seeking to refine your approach, this book offers strategies that can be implemented immediately.

Your Roadmap to Success

This book is structured to take you through the crucial aspects of managing small business taxes, providing a comprehensive toolkit. Each chapter builds upon the previous one, ensuring you gain a deep and practical understanding of every element needed to master your taxes and secure your business's financial health.

Chapter 1: Taming the Tax Beast

We'll break down the basics of small business taxes, including the different types of taxes you'll encounter and how your business structure impacts your tax obligations.

Chapter 2: The Devil's in the Details

You'll learn how to maintain accurate financial records that make the tax season less stressful and also help you make informed business decisions.

Chapter 3: Navigating Income Tax Returns

A walkthrough of the tax forms required for different business structures, helping you avoid common pitfalls and mistakes and enabling you to maximize your deductions.

Chapter 4: Understanding Your Tax Liability

Figure out exactly how much you owe in taxes! We'll provide the tools to calculate your taxes accurately and explore how deductions, credits, and business income affect your overall tax burden.

Chapter 5: The Taxman Cometh:

From sales to property tax, we'll guide you through the maze of taxes that vary by location, helping you stay compliant.

Chapter 6: In the Trenches:

Practical steps to file taxes efficiently and troubleshoot common issues, such as missing records or handling audits.

Chapter 7: Loopholes, Deductions, and Legal Magic

Explore advanced tactics, like leveraging legal loopholes, maximizing deductions, and taking complete advantage of tax credits.

Chapter 8: Help Is at Hand

Learn when and how to seek the assistance of CPAs and tax services, ensuring you get expert advice without having to overpay for it.

Chapter 9: The More You Know

Resources and strategies for staying informed so you can adapt your tax strategies as laws and regulations evolve. Plus, we'll dive into predicted tax trends that may impact your business..

Chapter 10: Beyond Taxes

Taxes are just one part of your financial responsibilities. This chapter covers the basics of bookkeeping and accounting, to ensure your business has a solid and sustainable financial foundation.

Meet Your Guides: The Expertise Behind the Pages

Garrett Monroe is not a single author but rather a collective pen name representing a team of seasoned professionals who bring a wealth of expertise from various sectors, including business, accounting, financial planning, and entrepreneurship.

The Garrett Monroe team has successfully guided countless entrepreneurs through the challenges of managing their business finances, ensuring they are compliant with tax regulations and positioned for long-term success. With a proven track record in helping small businesses thrive, Garrett Monroe is dedicated to providing you with tools needed to succeed.

Now, as you start your journey through the intricacies of small business taxes, remember that knowledge is your greatest asset. Taking control of your financial future starts here!

CHAPTER 1

Taming the Tax Beast: The Basics of Small Business Taxes

"The hardest thing in the world to understand is the income tax."
–Albert Einstein, World-renowned physicist.

Exploring the Four General Types of Business Taxes

Unraveling Income Tax: The Tax You Can't Escape

Income tax is an unavoidable part of running a small business..
Whether you're operating as a sole proprietorship, an LLC, or a
corporation, it's imperative for you to understand your income tax
obligations to maintain compliance and avoid costly penalties. Income
tax is calculated on your business profits, so it is important to
accurately report all your income and take full advantage of available
deductions to help reduce your tax liability. To accurately report
income, it is essential to keep thorough records. Every dollar your
business earns must be documented, whether it's from sales, services,
or through other income sources. This income is then reported on
your tax return, typically through forms such as Schedule C, which is
for sole proprietors to report profits or losses, or Form 1120 which is
used by corporations to declare their income, gains, losses, and
deductions. Failing to report all of your income, or reporting it
inaccurately, can result in audits and/or penalties.

Deductions are the flip side of the coin. The IRS allows certain business expenses to be deducted from your taxable income, which lowers the amount of tax you owe.. Common deductions include operating expenses, office supplies, and even a portion of your home if you use it for business purposes. It's important to understand which deductions you qualify for and keep detailed records to support your claims. By properly managing your income reporting and deductions, you can legally minimize your overall tax liability.

The Ins & Outs of Self-Employment Tax

Self-employed individuals, including sole proprietors and members of LLCs, have an additional tax obligation known as the 'Self-employment tax', which covers Social Security and Medicare contributions. This differs from how traditional employees of larger corporations file their taxes because they split them with their employer. self-employed individuals, on the other hand,are responsible to pay the full amount – currently 15.3% of net earnings. This amount is split into 12.4% for Social Security and 2.9% for Medicare.

It's important to note that only the first $168,600 of your net earnings is subject to the Social Security portion of the self-employment tax, the amount of which is adjusted annually. , The Medicare tax applies to all of your earnings with an additional 0.9% imposed on net earnings exceeding $200,000 for single filers or $250,000 for joint filers.

The self-employment tax is calculated on net income, which is your gross income minus allowable business expenses. It's important to note that while business expenses can be deducted to reduce your taxable income, the self-employment tax is still applied to any remaining profit. This tax must be reported on Schedule SE, which is filed alongside your annual tax return. The IRS requires self-employed individuals to pay this tax quarterly, based on estimated earnings. Failure to make timely payments may result in penalties. Lastly, don't forget that you can deduct up to half of your taxable adjusted gross income when calculating self-employment tax.

The Purpose of Excise Taxes and Why You Have to Pay Them

Excise taxes are the specific type of tax levied on certain goods, services, and activities, distinct from general sales taxes. Unlike general sales taxes, which are applied broadly, excise taxes target particular products or transactions, often to discourage certain behaviors or to generate revenue for specific government programs. Businesses involved in producing, selling, or using these goods and services may also be subject to excise taxes.

Industries commonly affected by excise taxes include alcohol, tobacco, fuel, and transportation. For example,if a business sells alcohol, it will be required to pay federal excise taxes on each gallon sold. Similarly, companies that manufacture or import tobacco products are also subject to excise taxes. The transportation industry also incurs excise taxes on airline tickets or heavy trucks, the tax of which is often passed on to consumers as part of the purchase price.

Excise taxes may also apply to certain activities, such as environmental taxes levied on businesses that emit specific pollutants or penalties for non-compliance with specific regulations. The amount of excise tax owed typically depends upon the quantity of products sold or the activity performed rather than on overall revenue or income.

Employment Taxes: Payroll and FICA

If your business has employees, you'll need to be aware of employment taxes, including both payroll taxes and Federal Insurance Contributions Act (FICA) taxes. As an employer, you are required to withhold a portion of your employees' wages and contribute a matching amount.

Payroll tax withholdings encompass a range of deductions including federal income tax, state income tax (where applicable), and FICA taxes. FICA taxes have been specifically designed to fund Social Security and Medicare, which provide benefits to retired workers, differently-abled individuals with, and others in need. The total FICA tax rate is 15.3% of an employee's gross wages— —7.65% is withheld from the employee's paycheck and the remaining 7.65% is paid by the employer. In simpler terms,x for every dollar of an employee's wage, 15.3 cents go toward FICA taxes, half of which is covered by the business.

FICA taxes impact both employers and employees. For employers, these taxes are a significant cost of doing business and must be accurately calculated and reported to the IRS. Mismanaging payroll taxes can lead to severe consequences including significant penalties, interest charges, or even potential legal issues. For an employee, these taxes will reduce your take-home-pay, but provide valuable benefits to you when you get older.

How Your Business Structure Impacts Your Tax Burden

Sole Proprietorships as a Straightforward and Effective Strategy

A sole proprietorship is an excellent choice of a business structure for entrepreneurs, as it is highly straightforward and widely adopted. It constitutes an ideal choice for entrepreneurs who wish to start a business without establishing a corporation or partnership. In this setup, the owner and the business are legally considered the same entity, meaning the owner is personally responsible for all debts and liabilities the business incurs. Business income is reported directly on the owner's personal tax return, through Schedule C (Form 1040).

What makes a sole proprietorship a great option is its simplicity. There are no separate business taxes to file, and the owner retains all profits. However, this structure also presents certain challenges, particularly regarding liability and taxation. As the sole owner, you are personally liable for everything, which means your assets are up for grabs if the business faces debts or runs into legal issues. Additionally, sole proprietors are subject to self-employment tax, which can significantly increase their tax burden compared to other business structures.

Despite these challenges, sole proprietorships are an attractive option for small-scale setups where simplicity and direct control are prioritized. As the business continues to grow, the owner may want to consider other structures offering liability protection and tax advantages.

Sharing the Wealth (and the Tax Burden) through Partnerships

In a partnership, profits and losses are directly passed to the partners and reported on their individual tax returns, making this an appealing structure for those who want to share both the responsibilities and rewards of business ownership. The partnership itself does not pay income tax. Instead, it files an informational return (Form 1065) to report the income, deductions, and other financial details to the IRS. Each partner receives a Schedule K-1, which details their share of the partnership's income, deductions, and credits.

One of the primary benefits of a partnership is the pooling of resources and expertise, potentially leading to greater business success. However, partnerships come with their challenges, particularly regarding tax implications and liability. Each partner is personally liable for the debts and obligations of the business. This means that one partner's financial or legal troubles can affect the entire partnership. In addition, disputes over profit distribution and business management can complicate the relationship.

LLCs Bringing The Best of Both Worlds?

Limited Liability Companies (LLCs) are a popular choice amongst small business owners because they offer both flexibility in taxation and personal liability protection. Like corporations, LLCs provide limited liability benefits, protecting owners from personal responsibility for the company's debts. Unlike corporations, though,they benefit from the added advantage of profits passing directly to the owners' personal tax returns, thus avoiding the double taxation that C corporations do encounter. As a result, the LLC itself doesn't pay federal income taxes. Instead, any profits or losses are reported on the owners' individual tax returns.

A significant advantage for LLC owners is the Qualified Business Income (QBI) deduction, introduced by the 2017 Tax Cuts and Jobs Act (TCJA). This enables eligible LLC owners to deduct up to 20% of their QBI from their taxable income, which lowers their overall tax obligation. However, this deduction comes with certain limitations based on the type of business and the owner's income level

An important reminder – the QBI deduction is set to expire after 2025 unless Congress extends it or makes it permanent. The potential expiration of this deduction could significantly impact LLCs and other pass-through entities, as it would effectively increase their tax liability. Thus, many business owners and advocates are pushing for the deduction to be extended or made permanent.

Corporations: Double Taxation or Tax Shelter?

Corporations, specifically C corporations, are distinct due to their status as separate legal entities. While the separation can provide liability protection to the owners or shareholders, it does subject the corporation to double taxation. This occurs because profits are first taxed at the corporate level, and then shareholders are taxed again on any dividends when they report them on their personal tax returns.

While double taxation is often seen as a disadvantage, corporations also benefit from a permanently reduced corporate tax rate of 21%, a significant decrease from the previous 35% rate prior to the Tax Cuts and Jobs Act (TCJA) of 2017. This lower rate can be particularly advantageous for businesses that plan to reinvest profits back into the company rather than distribute them as dividends, effectively using the corporation as a tax shelter to retain earnings.

For small businesses with substantial income, incorporating can provide a structured way to manage profits, taxes, and growth.

S Corporations: A Special Tax Breed

S Corporations combine the benefits of a corporate structure with the advantages of pass-through taxation, making them appealing to small business owners. Similar to C corporations, S corporations offer shareholders liability protection, but they differ by allowing profits to flow directly to shareholders, who report the income on their personal tax returns, thus avoiding double taxation. This pass-through treatment is similar to that of LLCs and partnerships but with the added benefit of allowing shareholders to potentially qualify for the Qualified Business Income (QBI) deduction.

Eligible S corporation shareholders can use the QBI deduction, up to 20% from their taxable income. This deduction has been a significant tax-saving tool for many S corporations.

Estimated Taxes: Paying as You Go

Estimated Taxes: Who Needs to Pay and When

If you do not have taxes withheld automatically from your income, like with self-employed individuals, business owners, and freelancers, you must figure out your estimated taxes. If you expect to owe more than $1,000 when you file your return, the IRS will generally require that you pay your estimated taxes throughout the year.

Different business structures have varying responsibilities. For instance, in a sole proprietorship or partnership, the individual owners must pay estimated taxes on their share of the income. In contrast, S corporations may need to pay estimated taxes on behalf of the corporation if they expect to owe a substantial amount.

Calculating Your Estimated Taxes

There are a few steps to calculating your estimated taxes. First, start by estimating your expected income, including all sources of business revenue. Next, subtract any deductions and credits you anticipate claiming, such as business expenses or the QBI deduction. The final amount here is your taxable income, the number you will need to calculate your estimated taxes due.

To calculate your estimated taxes, use the tax rate that applies to your income level and business structure. For self-employed individuals, don't forget to include self-employment tax, which is 15.3% of your net income. Once you have your total tax liability, divide it by four to determine your quarterly estimated tax payments.

Several tools and resources can help simplify this process. The IRS provides Form 1040-ES, which includes a worksheet for calculating estimated taxes and payment vouchers. Additionally, online tax calculators, such as those offered by TurboTax or QuickBooks, can automatically calculate based on your input. You can also adjust your estimates throughout the year if there are any significant changes.

Paying Your Estimated Taxes: Avoiding Penalties

The IRS imposes penalties on taxpayers who underpay their estimated taxes, even if the underpayment is unintentional. These penalties can accumulate quickly.

If you underestimate your taxes and have to pay the penalty, it's generally calculated based on the amount of the underpayment, how long the payment should have been due for, and the interest rate set by the IRS. To avoid penalties, you should aim to pay at least 90% of your current year's tax liability or 100% of your previous year's tax liability, whichever is lower. For higher-income earners, those with adjusted gross incomes above $150,000, the threshold is 110% of the previous year's tax liability.

To avoid penalties, ensure your estimated tax payments are spread evenly across the four payment periods. If your income fluctuates throughout the year, the IRS allows for an annualized income installment method, which calculates your estimated taxes based on actual income earned in each period rather than dividing your annual estimate by four.

Adjusting Your Estimated Taxes When Life Changes

Life and business circumstances can change rapidly, impacting your income and, consequently, your estimated tax payments. Whether you experience a significant increase in business revenue, a decrease in income, or major life events like marriage, the birth of a child, or the sale of a business asset, adjusting your estimated taxes can help with underpayment or overpayment.

To adjust your estimated taxes, revisit your income projections for the year. If your income has increased, you'll likely need to increase your estimated payments to avoid a large tax bill at the end of the year. If your income has decreased, you can reduce your estimated payments, freeing up cash flow for other business needs. The IRS Form 1040-ES worksheet can help you recalculate your estimated tax liability based on your updated income figures.

In addition to income changes, consider any new deductions or credits you may be eligible for due to life changes. For example, if you've added a new dependent, you may qualify for additional credits that could reduce your overall tax liability. Keep in mind that significant changes, such as the sale of major assets, may require a one-time adjustment to your estimated payments rather than an ongoing change.

Examples of How Different Businesses Handle Their Taxes

Jane's Story: Taxes as a Sole Proprietor

Jane owns a small freelance graphic design business and operates as a sole proprietor. Jane tracks her income and expenses every year, understanding that her business earnings will be reported on her personal tax return using Schedule C. She knows that accurate record-keeping will help her maximize her deductions, which include home office expenses, software subscriptions, and supplies. However, Jane also faces the challenge of paying self-employment tax, which covers Social Security and Medicare.

By setting aside a portion of her income each month, Jane makes sure she has enough funds to cover her quarterly estimated tax payments. Her disciplined approach to managing her taxes has kept her compliant with IRS regulations and allowed her to avoid unexpected tax bills.

Bob and Sue's Story: Partnering Up and Splitting the Tax Burden

Bob and Sue co-own a small bakery in their hometown, operating as a general partnership. They agreed to share profits, losses, and tax responsibilities from the start equally. Each year, their bakery files Form 1065, the partnership tax return, which outlines the business's income, deductions, and credits. Bob and Sue then receive Schedule K-1 forms, detailing their respective shares of the bakery's income, which they report on their personal tax returns.

By working closely with a tax advisor, Bob and Sue have effective tax planning strategies to manage their tax burden while reinvesting profits into growing their business.

Acme LLC's Story: The Tale of an LLC in Tax Season

Acme LLC is a boutique consulting firm specializing in digital marketing strategies. Founded by two entrepreneurs, Sarah and David, Acme LLC has grown steadily over the past few years. As an LLC, the profits are distributed to Sarah and David, who report their shares on their individual tax returns.

Acme LLC carefully reviews its financials during tax season to maximize deductions, including business travel, office expenses, and marketing software. In addition, they can use the Qualified Business Income (QBI) deduction, allowing them to reduce their taxable income by 20%.Acme LLC's proactive tax planning and strategic use of deductions highlight the benefits of LLC flexibility during tax season.

Mega Corp's Story: A Corporation's Tax Journey

Mega Corp, a mid-sized manufacturing company, faces the responsibility of corporate taxation. After the company's profits get taxed at the corporate level, dividends distributed to shareholders are taxed again on their personal tax returns. However, Mega Corp has turned this potential disadvantage into an opportunity by reinvesting a substantial portion of its profits back into the business, thus minimizing the impact of dividend taxation.

The company also benefits from the permanently reduced corporate tax rate of 21%, introduced by the Tax Cuts and Jobs Act of 2017, which has significantly lowered its overall tax liability. By managing its taxable income and leveraging tax credits for research and development, Mega Corp effectively uses its corporate structure as a tax shelter.

Key Takeaways

- **The Four Types of Business Taxes:** Understanding income tax, self-employment tax, excise tax, and employment taxes is key when managing your business's tax obligations.

- **How Business Structure Affects Taxes:** The business structure you select—whether it's a sole proprietorship, partnership, LLC, or corporation—directly impacts your tax obligations.

- **Importance of Estimated Taxes:** Regularly paying and accurately calculating estimated taxes is crucial to avoiding penalties and maintaining healthy cash flow throughout the year.

- **Potential Changes to the QBI Deduction:** The Qualified Business Income (QBI) deduction has been a significant tax-saving tool for pass-through entities, but its potential expiration after 2025 could affect many businesses.

- **Proactive Tax Planning:** Proactive and strategic tax planning, including regular reviews of your financial situation and adjusting estimated taxes, is necessary for long-term business success and tax efficiency.

Buyer Bonus

As a way of saying thank you for your purchase, we're giving you our "*7-Figure Business Toolkit*" that includes six FREE downloads that are exclusive to our book readers!

Here's what you'll get:

1. **The Negotiation Mastery Cheat Sheet** – Master the art of negotiation and get a massive edge in your business.

2. **The Start Your LLC Checklist** – This step-by-step PDF shows you exactly how to get your LLC up and running.

3. **The Top 7 Websites To Start Your LLC** – Save hours on research and choose the best website to start your LLC.

4. **The Mindfulness Hacks for Entrepreneurs PDF** – Stay cool, calm, and collected through all the ups and downs of your business journey.

5. **The Small Biz Tax Deduction Checklist** – An easy checklist for the most common small business tax deductions.

6. **The IRS Audit Survival Guide** – Discover exactly what to do if the IRS comes knocking for an audit of your business.

To download your 7-Figure Business Toolkit, you can go to monroemethod.com/taxes or simply scan the QR code below:

CHAPTER 2

The Devil's in the Details: Record Keeping for Smooth Sailing at Tax Time

"The secret of success is to do the common things uncommonly well."
- John D. Rockefeller, massive entrepreneur and one of the wealthiest U.S. persons of all-time.

Why Detailed Record-Keeping Matters

The IRS Audit: Be Prepared, Not Scared

An IRS audit is one of the scariest prospects for any business owner - but with good recordkeeping, you can reduce the fear around it. The IRS typically audits businesses when there are discrepancies or red flags in their tax returns, such as larger-than-usual deductions, underreported income, or unusually high expenses. By maintaining detailed records of every financial transaction, from income to expenses, you can provide the documentation to support your claims.

Detailed records mean you are transparent with your records and accurate, which can expedite the audit process and potentially lead to a favorable outcome. Poorly maintained or incomplete records can result in fines, penalties, or even unexpected tax liabilities. Businesses that maintain organized records, including receipts, invoices, bank statements, and payroll records, can better respond to IRS inquiries, minimizing the disruption to their operations and allowing more time to focus on growing the business.

Why Every Receipt & Invoice Counts

While it may seem tedious to keep track of small expenses, those seemingly insignificant amounts can add up to substantial deductions over the course of a year. The IRS requires businesses to provide documentation for deductions claimed on their tax returns, and receipts are a huge part of that documentation. Without them, you may lose out on valuable deductions.

Every receipt serves as proof of a legitimate business expense, whether for office supplies, meals with clients, or travel expenses. It's not just about large purchases; even the cost of a cup of coffee purchased during a business meeting is deductible, provided you have the receipt to prove it. In the event of an audit, having your receipts can make the difference between a smooth resolution and a costly penalty. You should develop a habit of keeping and organizing receipts, no matter how small the expense, so that you can claim every deduction you're entitled to. To make this process easier, consider using apps like Expensify or Receipt Bank, which allow you to quickly scan and organize your receipts digitally.

In addition to receipts, maintaining a consistent filing system for invoices is equally important. Whether you organize invoices chronologically, by client, or by service type, a well-organized invoicing system helps track payments and ensures easy access to documents during audits or financial reviews. It will simplify tax filing and support accurate financial record-keeping at the same time, helping you stay compliant with IRS requirements.

The Benefits of Meticulous Records

One of the most immediate advantages of good record-keeping is the ease of tax preparation. Compiling your tax return becomes a straightforward process when all financial transactions are accurately documented and well-organized. You can quickly access the information needed to calculate deductions, report income, and substantiate expenses, reducing the time and stress typically associated with tax season.

Plus, good record-keeping can help when looking for financing. Both lenders and investors need comprehensive financial data to evaluate the strength and sustainability of your business. By presenting organized and accurate records, you demonstrate professionalism and build trust, increasing your chances of securing some much-needed funds.

The Connection Between Record Keeping and Cash Flow

Good record-keeping helps maintain healthy cash flow, the lifeblood of any successful business. Cash flow refers to the movement of money in and out of your business, and keeping track of this flow is what you need to do to build a successful business that lasts. Detailed records allow you to monitor income and expenses closely, ensuring that you clearly understand your financial position at any given time.

By regularly updating and reviewing your records, you can spot potential cash flow issues before they become a bigger issue. For example, if your records show that receivables are consistently late, you can proactively improve collections and avoid cash shortages. Similarly, tracking expenses helps you identify areas where you may be overspending, allowing you to cut costs and improve profitability.

Additionally, keeping precise records enables you to project future cash flow by analyzing past data. This foresight helps you anticipate when and where funds will be necessary, allowing you to budget effectively for upcoming costs.

Essential Records for Tax Filing

Financial Statements: The Backbone of Your Tax Return

When preparing your tax return, financial statements like income statements, balance sheets, and cash flow statements are the primary source of information for calculating your taxable income, determining eligible deductions, and showing that all reported figures are accurate and complete.

For instance, an income statement outlines your business's revenue and expenses over a particular time frame, allowing you to calculate your net profit or loss—an important figure for accurate tax filing. The balance sheet provides a detailed list of your assets, liabilities, and equity. At the same time, the cash flow statement monitors the flow of cash into and out of your business, emphasizing liquidity and aiding in effective cash flow management.

Without accurate financial statements, you risk underreporting or overreporting your income, which could lead to errors, audits, and potential penalties.

Payroll Records: Not Just for Big Businesses

Many small business owners might assume that detailed payroll records are only necessary for large corporations, but this couldn't be further from the truth. Regardless of the size of your business, keeping payroll records is necessary for accurate tax reporting and legal compliance. Payroll records include employee names, Social Security numbers, wages paid, tax withholdings, and benefits provided.

For businesses that employ staff, payroll taxes, including federal income tax withholding, Social Security, and Medicare, are required. Accurate payroll records ensure these taxes are correctly calculated and reported, preventing underpayment or overpayment, which could lead to fines or penalties. Additionally, maintaining up-to-date payroll records helps prepare year-end tax forms like W-2s, which must be provided to employees and filed with the IRS.

Even if your business only employs a few people or utilizes independent contractors, payroll records are vital for substantiating deductions for salaries, wages, and payroll taxes. Small business owners must also track payroll to ensure compliance with labor laws and regulations, such as the Fair Labor Standards Act (FLSA). Whether you have two employees or two hundred, payroll records are indispensable to your business's tax and financial health.

The Importance of Inventory Records

Inventory records are necessary for any business dealing with physical products, as they directly impact tax reporting and overall business management. Accurate inventory tracking ensures that your cost of goods sold (COGS) is calculated correctly, which is needed to determine your taxable income. An error in your inventory records can lead to either underreporting or overreporting of income, which can result in significant tax implications.

Moreover, inventory records can provide insights into your business's operational efficiency. By regularly tracking inventory levels, you can identify slow-moving products, optimize stock levels, and reduce holding costs. Inaccurate inventory records can lead to stockouts, overstocking, and cash flow problems.

From a tax perspective, the IRS requires businesses to maintain detailed records of inventory purchases, sales, and year-end inventory counts. This information is used to substantiate your reported income and COGS.

The Lowdown on Depreciation Records

Depreciation is crucial in tax reporting for businesses that own significant long-term assets like equipment, vehicles, and property. It enables you to allocate the cost of these assets over their useful lifespan, thereby lowering your taxable income annually. However, to correctly claim depreciation, keeping thorough records of your depreciable assets is key.

Depreciation records should include the date of purchase, the asset's original cost, its expected useful life, and the method of depreciation used (e.g., straight-line or declining balance). These records are needed to calculate the annual depreciation deduction and determine the asset's adjusted basis if you sell or dispose of it. The adjusted basis, in turn, affects your capital gains or losses.

Why You Should Care About Your Bank Statements

Bank statements are great tools for verifying your business's income and expenses. These statements provide an official record of all money flowing in and out of your business accounts, making them important for reconciling your books and ensuring accuracy in your financial reporting. Regularly reviewing your bank statements can catch discrepancies, identify unauthorized transactions, and ensure that all business expenses and revenues are accounted for.

The Role of Previous Tax Returns in Current Filings

Previous tax returns can be valuable tools as well. By reviewing past returns, you can identify recurring deductions, carryover losses, or credits that may still apply. These returns also provide a baseline for comparing year-over-year financial performance, helping to spot trends or anomalies that need further investigation. Additionally, readily available past returns is essential in case the IRS raises any questions about prior filings. Consistency in tax reporting is step one for avoiding red flags that could trigger audits, making previous tax returns a critical reference point in your tax preparation process.

Tools to Simplify Your Record Keeping

Embracing Technology: AI Tools for the Modern Small Business

Technology can simplify and enhance the record-keeping processes. Artificial intelligence (AI) has revolutionized small business operations by providing tools that automate routine tasks, minimize errors, and save time. AI-driven solutions are specifically designed to enhance different aspects of record-keeping, including data entry and financial analysis.

A significant benefit of using AI in record-keeping is its capacity to learn and adjust to the specific needs of your business. For instance, AI tools like QuickBooks Online Advanced and Xero can automatically categorize expenses, track invoices, and even flag potential discrepancies in your records. These tools can also integrate with your existing accounting software, providing real-time insights into your financial health and helping you make informed decisions.

Additionally, AI-powered tools can automate tasks such as generating financial reports, reconciling bank statements, and tracking tax deductions, reducing the time and effort required to maintain accurate records. Botkeeper, for example, combines AI and human expertise to manage bookkeeping tasks, allowing business owners to focus more on growth and less on administrative duties.

QuickBooks: The King of Small Business Accounting

QuickBooks has long been recognized as the go-to accounting software for small businesses, and for good reason. It offers a comprehensive suite of tools that simplify bookkeeping, payroll management, and tax preparation, making it easier for business owners to keep their finances in order. QuickBooks allows you to track income and expenses, manage invoices, and generate financial reports with just a few clicks.

One of the standout features of QuickBooks is its integration with various financial institutions, enabling automatic import of bank transactions, which streamlines the reconciliation process. Additionally, QuickBooks offers tax management tools that help you track deductible expenses, calculate estimated taxes, and generate the necessary forms for filing.

FreshBooks: A Fresh Take on Small Business Bookkeeping

FreshBooks has rapidly become popular among small business owners seeking a modern, user-friendly accounting solution. It is crafted with user-friendliness at its core, providing an intuitive interface that simplifies financial management, even for those without prior accounting experience. The platform excels in automating tedious tasks like invoicing, tracking expenses, and monitoring time, allowing business owners to concentrate on expanding their operations. FreshBooks also offers comprehensive reporting tools that deliver insights into your business's financial health.

Wave: Riding the Free Software Wave

Wave offers an excellent suite of financial tools tailored for small businesses, freelancers, and entrepreneurs—all free. As one of the few truly free accounting software platforms available, Wave provides comprehensive features, including invoicing, expense tracking, and receipt scanning, making it an ideal solution for businesses on a tight budget.

Wave also offers payroll and payment processing services for a small fee, making it a versatile option for businesses as they grow.

Excel: The Old Reliable

Despite the rise of specialized accounting software, Excel remains a versatile and powerful tool for managing business records. Excel's flexibility allows small business owners to create customized spreadsheets tailored to their specific needs, whether for budgeting, tracking expenses, or managing payroll. Its features, such as formulas, pivot tables, and data analysis tools, make it possible to handle complex financial tasks precisely.

Excel is particularly valuable for businesses that require a high level of customization or those that prefer a hands-on approach to their financial management. Additionally, Excel's compatibility with various other software platforms means you can easily import and export data as needed. While it may lack some of the automation features of modern accounting software, Excel's reliability, and widespread availability continue to make it a trusted choice.

How Patagonia Leverages Technology for Record Keeping

Patagonia, the outdoor apparel company known for its commitment to environmental sustainability, has adopted advanced digital tools to streamline its record-keeping practices. The company uses Microsoft Dynamics 365, a powerful business management tool, to manage its financial operations efficiently.

By integrating Microsoft technologies into their systems, Patagonia ensures comprehensive tracking of transactions, inventory, and payroll across its global operations. This approach to record-keeping keeps them prepared for tax season and supports their transparent reporting in sustainability efforts. Patagonia's strategy demonstrates how leveraging modern technology can enhance financial accuracy and corporate responsibility, setting a benchmark for other businesses that balance profitability with ethical practices.

Record Keeping Checklist: Don't Miss Any Important Details

The Ultimate Checklist for Small Business Record-Keeping

Accurate and thorough records are needed for any small business's smooth operation and financial health. Below is a checklist to ensure you have all the documents organized and readily accessible:

1. **Financial Statements**: Include income statements, balance sheets, and cash flow statements. These provide an overview of your business's financial health and are needed for tax preparation.

2. **Receipts and Invoices**: Keep detailed records of all business expenses and income, categorized by type and date, to substantiate deductions and income reported on your tax returns.

3. **Bank Statements**: Regularly reconcile your bank accounts with your financial records to ensure accuracy and catch any discrepancies early.

4. **Payroll Records**: Include details of wages paid, tax withholdings, benefits provided, and any other compensation-related documents, even if you only have a few employees.

5. **Inventory Records**: Track your inventory's purchase, sale, and remaining stock to accurately calculate your cost of goods sold (COGS) and maintain proper stock levels.

6. **Depreciation Records**: Maintain a log of all depreciable assets, including their purchase date, cost, and the method of depreciation used.

7. **Tax Returns and Supporting Documents**: Keep copies of all filed tax returns along with the records used to prepare them,

such as income statements, receipts, and invoices, for at least seven years.

8. **Legal Documents**: Include contracts, business licenses, permits, and any other legal documents that pertain to your business operations.

Tracking Your Expenses: A Month-by-Month Guide

Staying on top of your expenses throughout the year helps with maintaining accurate financial records and ensuring a smooth tax filing process. A month-by-month tracking system can help you manage your finances effectively:

1. **Monthly Reconciliation**: At the end of each month, reconcile your bank and credit card statements with your expense records to catch any discrepancies early.

2. **Categorize Expenses**: Use accounting software to categorize expenses by type, such as office supplies, travel, or marketing. This will make it easier to identify deductible expenses at tax time.

3. **Review and Adjust**: Regularly review your monthly expenses to identify trends or areas where you can cut costs. Adjust your budget accordingly to stay on track with your financial goals.

4. **Digitize Receipts:** Utilize digital tools to scan and save receipts as expenses arise, ensuring they are organized and easily accessible when required.

Ensuring Your Records Are Ready for Tax Time

Preparing your records well before tax season can significantly reduce stress and ensure your tax filing goes smoothly. Here's how to get your records tax-ready:

1. **Organize by Category**: Ensure all your financial records are categorized by type, such as income, expenses, payroll, and

inventory. This organization will make compiling the necessary information for your tax return easier.

2. **Review for Accuracy**: Double-check all records for accuracy, particularly your financial statements, receipts, and invoices. Correct any discrepancies before filing your taxes.

3. **Compile Supporting Documents**: Gather all supporting documents, including receipts, invoices, bank statements, and payroll records, and ensure they align with your financial statements.

4. **Consult Your Accountant**: If you work with an accountant or tax professional, provide them with all organized records well before the filing deadline to allow for thorough review and preparation.

Uncommon Documents You Might Need

While most business owners are aware of the common records needed for tax filing, some less obvious documents could be needed during tax time:

1. **Canceled Checks**: These can serve as proof of payments for expenses or charitable contributions, especially when receipts are unavailable.

2. **Loan Documents**: Records of any business loans, including the agreement, payment history, and interest paid, are important for both tax deductions and audits.

3. **Lease Agreements**: Keeping a copy of the lease agreement can help substantiate rent expenses if you rent office space or equipment.

4. **Vehicle Logs**: If you use a vehicle for business purposes, maintaining a detailed log of business miles driven, along with maintenance records, can help justify mileage deductions.

5. **Home Office Expenses**: For those claiming a home office deduction, keep records of mortgage interest, utility bills, and maintenance costs related to the portion of your home used for business.

Key Takeaways

- **The Importance of Detailed Record Keeping:** Proper record-keeping is crucial for avoiding IRS issues, ensuring smooth tax preparation, and maintaining financial health.

- **Essential Records for Tax Filing:** Financial statements, receipts, payroll records, and other documents form the backbone of accurate tax filings and long-term financial management.

- **Leveraging Technology:** Modern tools like AI, QuickBooks, and FreshBooks can significantly simplify the process of maintaining accurate and accessible records.

- **Real-Life Application:** Patagonia's use of advanced technology for record-keeping demonstrates the benefits of meticulous documentation in both financial management and sustainability reporting.

- **Month-by-Month Tracking:** Regular, systematic tracking of expenses and income ensures that your records are always up-to-date and ready for tax season.

- **Preparation for Tax Time:** Being prepared with organized, accurate records is key to a smooth and successful tax filing experience.

Chapter 3

Navigating Income Tax Returns

Navigating Income Tax Returns
"The avoidance of taxes is the only intellectual pursuit that still carries any reward."
— John Maynard Keynes, a British economist known for his contributions to modern economic theory

Tax Form Basics for Small Businesses.

Schedule C

Schedule C is a key tax document for sole proprietors, enabling them to report business-specific income and expenses. This form is submitted alongside the individual's tax return (Form 1040). It is crucial for calculating the business's net profit or loss, which is then incorporated into the owner's overall taxable income.

Key Sections:

- **Income:** On Schedule C, all business income is reported, including earnings from sales, services, and any other business activities.

- **Expenses:** This section allows sole proprietors to deduct various business-related expenses, reducing their taxable income. These expenses can include costs for supplies, advertising, utilities, and more.

- **Net Profit or Loss:** The form calculates the net profit or loss of the business, by subtracting total expenses from total income. This amount is then transferred to Form 1040, which becomes part of the proprietor's overall taxable income.

The Schedule C simplifies the tax process for sole proprietors through the integration of business and personal tax reporting including the payment of self-employment taxes, which also includes Social Security and Medicare contributions.

Form 1120

Form 1120 is used by C corporations to report their income, gains, losses, deductions, and credits. Unlike sole proprietors, corporations are recognized as separate legal entities and are required to submit their own tax returns, distinct from those of their shareholders.

Key Sections:

- **Income:** Corporations must report all forms of income on Form 1120, including revenue from sales, dividends, along with other earnings. This income is taxed on abidance corporate tax rates, which are different from those applied to individuals.

- **Deductions:** Form 1120 allows corporations to deduct various business expenses, including employee salaries, rent, and interest on business loans. Deductions reduce the corporation's taxable income, lowering the overall tax liability.

- **Tax Computation:** The form includes a section to calculate the corporation's total taxable income after deductions. This amount is then used to determine the corporation's tax liability based on the current corporate tax rate, which was permanently reduced to 21% by the Tax Cuts and Jobs Act (TCJA) of 2017

Submitting Form 1120 enables corporations to utilize various deductions and credits that lower their tax liability. Nevertheless, corporations encounter the issue of double taxation, where income is taxed both at the corporate level and then once more at the time of dividend distribution to shareholders.

Form 1120-S

Form 1120-S is a tax document used by S Corporations to report their income, deductions, and credits. Unlike C Corporations, an S Corporation's structure allows for it to pass income directly to its shareholders, thereby eliminating a double taxation issue.

This form ensures that income is reported and allocated accurately to each individual shareholder based on their ownership percentage.

Key Sections:

- **Income and Deductions:** Form 1120-S requires reporting of the corporation's income and deductions just like other corporate tax forms. However, instead of paying corporate taxes, the net income or loss is divided among the shareholders and reported on their individual tax returns through Schedule K-1.

- **Schedule K-1:** One of the most unique aspects of Form 1120-S is Schedule K-1. This schedule distributes the corporation's income, deductions, and credits to shareholders based on their ownership percentage. Shareholders then report this information on their personal tax returns, ensuring that the income is taxed individually rather than at the corporate level.

- **Qualified Business Income (QBI) Deduction:** Shareholders of S Corporations may also benefit from the QBI deduction, which allows up to 20% deduction on qualified business income. Note that this deduction is subject to expiration after 2025, unless it is extended.

Form 1120-S provides S Corporations the advantage of significant tax savings with a way to pass income directly to shareholders. . However, the complexity of ensuring accurate allocation through Schedule K-1 and the potential changes to tax laws mean S Corporations need to stay informed.

How Business Structures Determine Forms

The structure of a business significantly impacts which tax forms need to be used for tax filing purposes. Every business structure— whether it's a sole proprietorship, partnership, LLC, or corporation— entails unique tax obligations and filing procedures.

Sole Proprietorships:

Sole proprietors generally submit Schedule C together with their personal Form 1040. This form integrates the owner's income and expenses of the business with their personal tax return, making it one of the simpler filing processes.

Partnerships:

Partnerships are required to submit Form 1065, which details the partnership's income, deductions, and credits. This income is subsequently passed on to the partners, who report it on their personal tax returns through Schedule K-1.

LLCs:

LLCs typically have more flexibility in taxation. A single-member LLC typically files Schedule C, while multi-member LLCs file as partnerships using Form 1065. LLCs can also elect to be taxed as a corporation, in which case they would file Form 1120 (C Corporation) or Form 1120-S (S Corporation).

Corporations:

C Corporations file Form 1120, paying taxes at the corporate level, while S Corporations file Form 1120-S, passing income to shareholders to eliminate double taxation. The choice between these forms depends on if the corporation has elected S Corporation status.

A Step-by-Step Guide to Filling Out Your Forms

Schedule C: Line by Line

Filling out Schedule C can seem daunting, but breaking it down line by line can simplify the process. Here's a step-by-step guide to help you confidently navigate through each section..

Step 1: General Information

- **Part I - Income:** Start by reporting your gross receipts or sales in Line 1. This is the total income generated by your business before any expenses have been deducted. If you offer returns or allowances, deduct them in Line 2, and report your net receipts in Line 3.

- **Line 7:** Calculate your gross income by deducting the cost of goods sold (Line 4) from your total net receipts. This amount is crucial as it determines your total taxable income.

Step 2: Expenses

- **Part II - Expenses:** This part addresses various deductible expenses related to your business. Common categories include advertising (Line 8), car and truck expenses (Line 9), and wages (Line 26). Each expense category should reflect actual business-related expenditures, backed by proper documentation.

- **Line 27a:** Deduct any other business expenses that don't fit into the specified categories in Line 27a. This can include items like professional fees, subscriptions, or educational expenses.

Step 3: Net Profit or Loss

- **Line 31:** Determine your net profit or loss by deducting your total expenses from your gross income. If you end up with a profit, this figure will be carried over to your Form 1040, adding to your overall taxable income. Conversely, if you incur a loss, it may enable you to offset other sources of income.

Final Tips:

- **Accuracy:** Double-check all entries to ensure they match your financial records. The IRS closely scrutinizes Schedule C filings.

- **Documentation:** Keep all supporting documents prepared, like receipts and invoices. Proper documentation can prevent disputes with the IRS and safeguard your deductions.

Form 1120 Walkthrough for Corporations

Form 1120 is the corporate income tax return filed by C Corporations. While more complex than Schedule C, if you follow a step-by-step process, it can seem easier. This guide will help you fill out the key sections and avoid common pitfalls.

Step 1: Income

- **Line 11 - Total Income:** Begin by reporting the corporation's gross income, including sales, services, and other revenue streams. Ensure that all income is reported for the corporation.

Step 2: Deductions

- **Part II - Deductions:** Corporations can deduct many expenses to reduce the taxable income. Common deductions include compensation of officers (Line 12), salaries and wages (Line 13), and repairs and maintenance (Line 14). It's important to accurately categorize each expense and ensure they are attributed to running the e business.

- **Line 27 - Other Deductions:** Use this line for miscellaneous deductions that don't fit into the predefined categories, such as legal fees or advertising costs.

Step 3: Tax Computation

- **Line 31 - Taxable Income:** Calculate the corporation's taxable income after accounting for all allowable deductions. This figure forms the basis for determining the corporation's federal income tax liability.

- **Line 35 - Total Tax:** Use the current corporate tax rate, which is 21% as per the TCJA, to compute the corporation's due tax. Ensure all credits and payments are properly accounted for to minimize tax liability.

Final Tips:

- **Avoiding Mistakes:** Common errors include underreporting income or overestimating deductions. Double-check figures and consult with a tax professional if it seems necessary.

- **Documentation:** Y. Accurate documentation of all transactions and deductions is essential for avoiding disputes with the IRS and ensuring compliance.

Form 1120-S: Making S Corporations Less Scary

Completing Form 1120-S can seem challenging. However, simplifying it into clear, manageable steps can be of help. S Corporations use this form to document their income, losses, deductions, and credits, which are passed on to shareholders for tax reporting purposes.

Key Sections:

- **Part I - Income:** Start by reporting total income, which includes gross revenue or sales, minus returns and allowances. Calculate the net income carefully, as errors here can lead to discrepancies in shareholder allocations.

- **Part II - Deductions:** Carefully list out deductions such as salaries, rents, and taxes that reduce the corporation's taxable income, impacting the income reported by shareholders on their personal returns.

Common Pitfalls:

- **Schedule K-1:** Ensure that the information on Schedule K-1 is accurate, as it determines what each shareholder reports on their individual tax returns. Errors in this section can lead to IRS audits for both the corporation and the shareholders.

- **Qualified Business Income (QBI) Deduction:** Don't forget the QBI deduction, which allows a 20% deduction on qualified business income. However, be mindful of its potential expiration after 2025.

Deductions: Maximizing Your Expenses

Deductions are a powerful tool for reducing taxable income, but it is important to understand which ones can be claimed and how their benefits can be maximized. This section provides insights into identifying and claiming the maximum allowable deductions on various tax forms.

Identifying Deductions:

- **Common Deductions:** On forms like Schedule C and Form 1120, you can deduct a wide range of business expenses, including rent, utilities, employee salaries, and marketing costs.

Keep good records and receipts to substantiate your claims to maximize these deductions.

- **Depreciation:** Remember to account for depreciation, which enables you to gradually deduct the cost of physical assets over their life. This deduction is particularly important for businesses with significant equipment or real estate investments.

Impact of TCJA Expiration:

- **Business Meals Deduction:** A key provision to watch is the potential expiration of the enhanced business meals deduction, which allowed accountance for 100% deduction on meals during the COVID-19 relief period. If the TCJA provisions expire after 2025, this deduction might revert to the pre-2018 rule, limiting it to 50%.

Income, Expenses, Depreciation

Accurately reporting income, expenses, and depreciation ensures compliance and optimization of tax outcomes. Here's how to approach these key elements across different tax forms.

Income Reporting:

- **Accuracy:** Report all income accurately, everything from sales to services or any other forms of revenue. Misreporting income can lead to penalties and increased scrutiny from the IRS.

Expenses:

- **Comprehensive Reporting:** Deduct all allowable business expenses, from office supplies to employee wages. Be thorough in categorizing these expenses on your tax forms to ensure you capture all potential deductions.

Depreciation:

- **Tangible Assets:** Use depreciation to spread the cost of tangible assets, like equipment and vehicles, over their expected useful life. This annual deduction can significantly reduce your taxable income.

Final Note:

- **Documentation:** Keep detailed records to support your income, expenses, and depreciation claims. Proper documentation is your best defense in the event of an audit.

Mistakes to Avoid When Filling Out Your Forms

Commonly Overlooked Deductions

Maximizing deductions is a key strategy for reducing your tax liability. Yet, many small business owners overlook the opportunity for valuable deductions.

Tips to Ensure You Don't Miss Out:

- **Home Office Deduction:** If a section of your home is dedicated solely to business use, you might be eligible for a home office deduction. This deduction permits you to claim a percentage of your mortgage, rent, utilities, and even insurance as part of business expenses.

- **Mileage Deduction:** To claim the mileage deduction, keep track of your business-related travel expenses. Use a reliable mileage tracker or app to ensure you don't miss out on this valuable deduction.

- **Business Meals and Entertainment:** Remember to deduct 50% of your business meals, and if they were during the

COVID-19 relief period, a temporary 100% deduction is allowed which may revert after 2025.

Final Tip:

- **Review Past Returns:** Look at previous tax returns to identify deductions you may have missed out on in prior years, and make sure to claim them in the upcoming tax season.

Misclassifying Income

Misclassifying income is a common mistake that can lead to underpayment of taxes and trigger IRS penalties.

Common Errors and How to Avoid Them:

- **Business vs. Personal Income:** Ensure that all business income is reported on the correct forms. For ease and simplicity, avoid mixing personal and business income.

- **Income Source:** Correctly classify different sources of income, such as: sales, services, and investments. Misclassifying income can affect your tax liability and eligibility for certain deductions.

Final Tip:

- **Consult with a CPA:** If you're unsure about income classification, seek advice from a qualified accountant to avoid costly mistakes.

Forgetting to Include All Forms and Schedules

Omitting required forms and schedules is a mistake that is frequently made. It can lead to longer return processing times, or even cause potential penalties to incur.

The Importance of Including All Forms:

- **IRS Requirements:** The IRS requires all relevant forms and schedules to be included with your return. Missing forms can result in an incomplete return, triggering an audit or leading to penalties.

- **Double-Check Your Return:** Review your tax return to make sure all required forms and schedules are included. A checklist will help make it easier.

Final Tip:

- **Electronic Filing:** Consider filing electronically. Tax software often provides prompts that ensure inclusion of all necessary forms and schedules.

Avoiding Calculation Catastrophes

Errors in calculations can lead to significant issues,such as an underpayment of taxes or triggering an IRS audit. Double-check your math to avoid costly mistakes.

How to Avoid Calculation Errors:

- **Use Tax Software:** Tax software like TurboTax automates calculations, reducing the risk of errors.

- **Manual Review:** Even if you use software, manually reviewing key calculations can catch mistakes that automated systems might miss.

- **Reconcile Accounts:** Ensure that your financial statements and bank records align with the numbers reported on your tax forms.

Final Tip:

- **Consult a Professional:** Consider consulting a tax professional to ensure the accuracy of complex calculations.

Late Filing

Late filing of tax returns can result in penalties and heavy interest, significantly increasing your tax burden.

Consequences of Late Filing:

- **Penalties:** The IRS imposes a penalty on unpaid taxes of between 5%-25% for each month or part of a month that a tax return is late.

- **Interest:** In addition to penalties, any unpaid taxes from the date they are due until their full payment, accrued interest.

Strategies to Ensure Timely Submission:

- **Set Reminders:** Use calendar alerts to remind you of key tax deadlines.

- **Organize Early:** Begin gathering necessary documents and information well before the filing deadline.

- **File for an Extension:** If you're unable to file on time, submit Form 4868 to request a six-month extension, but remember that this does not extend the time to pay any taxes already owed.

Final Tip:

- **Electronic Filing:** Consider filing electronically, as it ensures faster processing time and submission confirmation.

TurboTax and Small Business Tax Returns

TurboTax has become a trusted tool for many small business owners, thanks to its user-friendly interface and comprehensive tax filing guidance. A notable example of how TurboTax assisted a small marketing consultancy firm operating as an S Corporation by navigating the complexities of its tax returns. The firm used TurboTax's step-by-step guidance to complete Form 1120-S, ensuring accuracy and compliance.

How TurboTax Helped:

- **Error-Flagging:** TurboTax's software flagged potential errors, such as misclassified income and overlooked deductions, helping the consultancy avoid common filing mistakes.

- **Maximizing Deductions:** The platform's detailed deduction assistance ensured the business maximized its eligible deductions, including those business-related and depreciation expenses.

- **Real-Time Support:** TurboTax's real-time support feature provides small business owners with answers to specific tax questions, enhancing their understanding of tax obligations.

Key Takeaways

- **Understanding Tax Forms:** It's essential to know which tax forms are required for your specific business structure to ensure accurate filing.

- **Step-by-Step Guidance:** A structured approach to filling out tax forms can help to avoid mistakes and make the process less daunting overall.

- **Avoiding Common Mistakes:** Being aware of common errors, such as overlooking deductions or misclassifying income, can save you time and money.

- **Maximizing Deductions:** Understanding how to claim all allowable deductions is crucial for minimizing your tax liability. Note: Emphasize the importance of staying informed about changes like the potential expiration of TCJA provisions, which could impact deductions.

- **Importance of Timely Filing:** Late filing can lead to significant penalties, so staying on top of deadlines is essential.

- **Leveraging Technology:** Tools like TurboTax can streamline the tax filing process, making it easier for small businesses to meet their obligations accurately and efficiently.

CHAPTER 4

Understanding Your Tax Liability

"There may be liberty and justice for all, but there are tax breaks only for some."
— **Martin A. Sullivan, Economist and Tax Expert**

How Much Do Small Businesses Actually Pay in Taxes?

The Good, The Bad, and The Ugly of Tax Rates for Small Businesses

The type of business structure you choose for your business can dramatically change the tax rate and obligations. Here's what you can typically expect:

1. Sole Proprietorships:

Sole proprietors are taxed on their individual income tax returns, with an effective tax rate generally averaging around 13.3%. This varies by income level and the amount of deductions.

2. Partnerships and S Corporations:

These pass-through entities allow income to be taxed on the individual's personal tax return instead of at the corporate level. The effective tax rate for these businesses usually hovers around 23.6%. However, this may change depending on factors such as income levels and the use of available deductions and credits.

3. Traditional Corporations (C Corporations):

C corporations are subject to a flat corporate tax rate of 21%. However, this structure leads to double taxation, as dividends paid out to shareholders are also taxed as part of their personal income tax returns.

4. Individual Income Tax Rates:

Tax rates range from 10% to 37% for individuals, depending on the income bracket. For small business owners, particularly those who are self-employed, the self-employment tax adds another layer of complexity, as it covers Social Security and Medicare contributions at a rate of 15.3% of net earnings. Half of this self-employment tax is deductible on your income taxes, which creates an offset.

Slicing the Tax Pie on Federal, State, and Local Taxes

The tax obligations for small businesses include federal, state, and local taxes. At the federal level, businesses are primarily concerned with income taxes. The federal corporate tax rate was reduced to 21% under the Tax Cuts and Jobs Act (TCJA) of 2017, benefiting many businesses but introducing new rules with the Qualified Business Income (QBI) deduction for pass-through entities.

State taxes add another layer. Each state has its own tax laws, with some states charging income taxes, while others rely more heavily on sales taxes or property taxes. For example, businesses operating in states like California or New York face higher state income tax rates, while those in states like Florida or Texas, have no state income tax, but they do have other forms of taxation, such as higher property or sales taxes.

Local taxes can further complicate things. Cities and municipalities may impose their own taxes, including local income taxes, property taxes, and business license taxes. These taxes can vary widely, even within the same state.

For instance, a small retail business operating in New York City must navigate both federal income taxes, as well as New York State's corporate tax and New York City's unincorporated business tax. The state imposes a corporate income tax rate of 6.5%, and the city adds another layer of tax that can reach up to 4%. This combined amount, sales taxes, and potential property taxes have massive implications for small businesses in high-tax states like New York.

Effective vs. Marginal Tax Rates

Small business owners need to understand the difference between effective and marginal tax rates, as they impact financial strategy and long-term tax planning. Marginal Tax Rate: This is the rate applied to your last dollar of income. It is determined through a progressive tax system, which segments income into various tax brackets, each with a distinct tax rate. A small business in the United States that earns $50,000 in taxable income might fall into a lower tax bracket, say at 12%, whereas if the income increases to $100,000, part of that *additional* income may be taxed at a higher rate, say at 22%.

Effective Tax Rate: In contrast, the effective tax rate represents the average percentage of your total income that is paid in taxes. It's calculated by dividing the total taxes paid by your overall taxable income. If a business pays $20,000 in taxes on $100,000 of taxable income, its effective tax rate is 20%, even though the business's marginal tax rate might be much higher. This effective rate provides a more accurate picture of the overall tax burden since it accounts for all income and tax brackets rather than just the highest bracket the business falls into.

Importance for Tax Planning: Knowing your marginal and effective tax rate assists in tax planning. While the marginal rate shows the tax impact of earning additional income, the effective rate provides a broader perspective on overall tax liability. Knowing these rates, you can leverage them through managing your income and deductions, lowering your effective tax rate, reducing your overall tax burden, and freeing up more capital for investment and growth purposes. Moreover, through a comprehensive understanding of marginal rates, you may be able to time income and expenses in a manner that minimizes the tax impact, especially as income nears a higher tax bracket or it is the corporate year-end.

Factors That Influence Your Tax Liability

Your Business Structure and Its Impact on Taxes

The type of business structure you choose plays an important role in determining your tax obligations. Taxation varies significantly between different business structures such as sole proprietorships, partnerships, LLCs, and corporations. For instance, sole proprietors report business income on their personal tax returns, which means that individual income tax rates are applied to the income subject to self-employment tax.

Income is reported on the tax returns of individual partners or members in the case of partnerships and LLCs, often considered as pass-through entities. This allows profits to 'pass-through' to owners without them being subject to corporate income tax. However, self-employment taxes are still mandated. Hence, each member's share of income, deductions, and credits need to be meticulously kept track of.

Corporations are unique because they face double taxation—first on the corporate income at a flat rate of 21% and then again, when dividends are paid to shareholders who report them as part of their personal tax returns. S Corporations, though also pass-through entities, can avoid double taxation by allowing income to pass through directly to shareholders, but they must meet specific IRS requirements to maintain this status.

How Your State Can Tax You Based on Your Location

State-specific tax laws can dramatically influence your small business's tax liability. States like California, New York, and New Jersey are known for their high tax rates, including state income taxes, sales taxes, and additional business taxes. These taxes can quickly increase the overall tax burden for businesses operating in these regions.

For example, let's look at a tech startup company in California, a state with high taxes. This startup faces a state corporate income tax rate of 8.84% and has additional tax liabilities, such as the minimum franchise tax, which is required regardless of profitability. The startup must pay these high taxes while trying to remain competitive in a fast-paced industry. In contrast, a similar startup in Texas with no state income tax might have more flexibility in reinvesting profits back into the business.

How Business Income Speeds Up Your Tax Meter

As your business income grows, so does your tax liability. Proactively managing income through strategies like deferring income, accelerating deductions, and taking advantage of credits can help ease the impact of rising tax rates.

Deductions: Your Secret Weapon

Deductions can really reduce liability. By carefully tracking and documenting common deductions such as expenses for home office use, business travel, office supplies, and employee salaries can help to lower your taxable income and save you money on your tax bill.

Credits: The Tax World's Golden Tickets

Tax credits lower your tax bill directly, making them more beneficial than deductions. For instance, the Work Opportunity Tax Credit

(WOTC) encourages businesses to employ individuals from specific groups, including veterans or those facing substantial employment challenges.

For example, a small business owner in the hospitality industry hired several veterans, which qualified them for the WOTC. By claiming this credit, they reduced their tax liability by thousands of dollars, lowering their overall tax burden. Credits like these are great tools in tax planning, offering huge savings and sometimes even creating a situation where the business owes little to no tax.

Capital Gains and Losses: Tax Effects on the Long- and Short-Term

Capital gains and losses from the sale of assets like stocks, real estate, or business equipment can play a significant role in determining your overall tax liability. Long-term capital gains, earned from assets held over a year, benefit from a reduced tax rate, whereas short-term gains, from assets held for under a year, are subject to the higher standard income tax rate.

Strategic management of these gains and losses can impact your taxes, offsetting gains with losses (which is called tax-loss harvesting) can reduce taxable income.

A Sample Tax Liability Calculation

Let's consider a small graphic design business, 'Design Co.,' with a total annual income of $100,000. After deducting $20,000 in business expenses, such as office supplies, software subscriptions, and travel, the taxable income is reduced to $80,000.

Assuming the business is structured as an LLC and qualifies for the Qualified Business Income (QBI) deduction, it can further reduce taxable income by 20%, or $16,000, bringing it down to $64,000. If

Design Co. is eligible for a $2,500 tax credit, such as through the Work Opportunity Tax Credit, then the final tax liability would be calculated based on the $64,000 minus the $2,500 credit.

Zero to Hero: Calculating Your Tax Liability

Step-by-Step Guide to Calculating Taxes

There are several steps you can take to calculate your taxes:

1. **Determine Gross Income:**

   o Add up all revenue streams to determine your total gross income.

2. **Subtract Allowable Deductions:**

   o Deduct operating expenses and other eligible deductions to calculate your taxable income.

3. **Apply Tax Rates:**

   o Apply the relevant federal tax rates to your taxable income to find your preliminary tax liability.

4. **Factor in Tax Credits:**

   o Subtract any tax credits that your business qualifies for, as these directly reduce the amount of tax owed.

5. **Add State and Local Taxes:**

   o Include any applicable state and local taxes to determine your total tax liability.

6. **Use Tools for Accuracy:**

   o Using tax software or speaking and engaging with a tax professional can help to avoid errors and ensure accuracy.

How Your Operating Income Affects Your Taxes

Operating income is a key factor in determining your overall tax liability. The more profit your business generates, the higher your taxable income, which could push you into a higher tax bracket. This makes it crucial for you to manage your operating income effectively by considering the timing of income recognition and strategic investments as part of deductible expenses to lower your taxable income. Understanding the relationship between operating income and taxes allows you to make decisions that optimize your tax outcomes.

How Deductions and Credits Change the Story

Deductions and credits can help to reduce your tax liability. While deductions lower your taxable income, credits directly reduce the amount of tax you owe. For instance, a $1,000 deduction might save you $250 in taxes if you're part of the 25% tax bracket, whereas a $1,000 tax credit would reduce your tax bill by $1,000 overall. For help in estimating your tax liability, refer to some of the tools provided at the back of the book.

Ben & Jerry's and Their Progressive Tax Approach

Ben & Jerry's Homemade Holdings Inc.

Ben & Jerry's, the iconic ice cream company, has long been recognized for its delicious flavors and commitment to social responsibility. In the early years, co-founders Ben Cohen and Jerry Greenfield implemented a unique approach to managing their corporate tax liability by advocating for a progressive corporate tax rate within their company. They established a policy where the highest-paid employee would not earn more than five times the salary of the lowest-paid employee. This approach directly impacted their corporate tax obligations, reducing their overall tax burden while aligning with their ethical values.

Key Takeaways

- **Average Tax Rates:** Understanding the average tax rates for small businesses can help you better anticipate your tax burden.

- **Federal, State, and Local Taxes:** Your total tax liability includes more than just federal taxes; state and local taxes also play a significant role.

- **Effective vs. Marginal Tax Rates:** Knowing the difference between effective and marginal tax rates can aid in more accurate tax planning.

- **Impact of Business Structure:** Your business structure significantly affects your tax obligations, influencing which forms you must file and your overall tax rate.

- **Deductions and Credits:** Strategic use of deductions and credits can substantially lower your tax liability, but staying informed about potential changes in tax law, such as the expiration of TCJA provisions, is crucial.

- **Proactive Tax Calculation:** Regularly calculating your tax liability helps avoid surprises and prepares you for tax season.

CHAPTER 5

The Taxman Cometh: Paying State and Local Taxes

"Taxes are the price we pay for a civilized society."
— **Oliver Wendell Holmes Jr., a former Associate Justice of the Supreme Court of the United States**

Common State and Local Tax Requirements

Understanding Each State's Tax Landscape

Every state has its own tax laws, with varying rules and rates that can impact businesses. Moreover, states vary in their handling of property, sales, and excise taxes. Businesses need to be aware of these differences and understand the specific tax obligations in the states where they operate. These can influence everything from pricing strategies to the firm's overall profitability.

Income Taxes: Not Just a Federal Matter

State income taxes are generally cumbersome, especially for companies with operations spread across multiple states. Unlike federal taxes, which are uniform country-wide, state income taxes vary and are determined by the state in which the business operates. Certain states apply a flat tax rate, whereas others implement a progressive tax structure.

Sales Tax: The Invisible Hand in Every Transaction

Sales tax is a big component of doing business, especially for companies that sell goods or services directly to consumers. The rate and application of sales tax can differ widely across different states, and even within the same states as local jurisdictions may impose additional sales taxes. Businesses are required to collect the correct amount of sales tax from customers and submit it to the state.

Property Taxes: Owning a Piece of the Rock Has Its Price

Property taxes are another significant expense for businesses that own real estate. These taxes are determined by the value of a particular property and may be impacted based on the location. Some states and localities have higher property tax rates, which can affect decisions about where to locate a business.

Excise Taxes: Hidden Costs You May Be Overlooking

Excise taxes are often overlooked but can represent a substantial cost for businesses in specific industries, such as those dealing in alcohol, tobacco, or fuel. These taxes are generally applied to the sale of certain goods and can vary depending on both the state and the type of product.

Navigating Employment Taxes

Payroll Taxes: More Than Just a Line on a Paycheck

Payroll taxes are a mandatory part of employee compensation. These taxes include both federal income tax withholding as well as Social Security and Medicare contributions, which must be deducted from employees' paychecks. Additionally, employers are responsible for matching the Social Security and Medicare contributions, effectively doubling the amount paid into these programs. States may also have their own payroll taxes. To remain compliant and avoid penalties, businesses must accurately calculate and promptly remit payroll taxes.

Preparing for Rainy Days Through Unemployment Insurance Taxes

Unemployment insurance taxes form another big component of employment taxes. These taxes support state unemployment insurance programs, offering financial aid to workers who lose their jobs for reasons beyond their control. The unemployment insurance tax rate differs from state to state and is usually determined by the employer's history of claims and the state's current unemployment rate. Employers are required to pay this tax on behalf of their employees.

Workers' Compensation for Accidents

In most states, businesses are required to have workers' compensation insurance for their employees, which covers medical costs and lost wages if a workplace injury occurs. The expense of this insurance depends on factors like the industry, the type of work involved, and the company's claims history. Although not a tax in the traditional sense, workers' compensation premiums are a significant cost to businesses that they must incur. Not maintaining sufficient workers' compensation insurance can result in penalties, legal action, and, in some states, even criminal prosecution. Proper management of workers' compensation protects employees and shields businesses from potentially devastating financial liability.

The Double Punch from Federal and State Employment Taxes

Employment taxes present a dual challenge for businesses, as they must comply with both federal and state requirements. Federal employment taxes are standardized across the country, but state employment taxes can vary widely, with different rates, requirements, and filing deadlines. Managing this dual system necessitates thorough planning and precise record-keeping to ensure that all requirements are fulfilled promptly. Businesses must stay up to date with changes in tax laws at both levels, as non-compliance can result in significant penalties.

Checklist: Meeting Your State and Local Tax Obligations

The Ultimate State and Local Tax Checklist: Cover All Bases

To stay compliant with state and local tax requirements, a thorough checklist that covers all bases is necessary. **Here's a comprehensive guide that may help:**

1. **Register Your Business:** Make sure your business is registered with the appropriate state and local tax authorities. This typically involves obtaining a state tax ID number and, if applicable, registering for local business licenses.

2. **Know Your Filing Schedule:** Based on your state's regulations and the type of tax, your timeline for filing tax returns could be on a monthly, quarterly, or yearly basis. Maintain a detailed calendar to track all filing deadlines to ensure you never miss a due date.

3. **Sales Tax Management:** For businesses that sell taxable goods or services, proper registration to collect sales tax in every state where the business operates is essential. Regularly check and update your knowledge of tax rates and regulations in each area, and make sure to remit the collected sales taxes to the appropriate authorities in a prompt and timely manner.

4. **Track Payroll Taxes:** Stay on top of state payroll taxes, including state income tax withholding and unemployment insurance taxes.

   Make timely deposits and accurate reporting to avoid penalties.

5. **File Property Tax Returns:** If your business owns real estate or other taxable property, ensure your property tax returns are filed timely. Pay any due taxes by the mandated deadlines. Keep detailed records of assessed values and payments.

6. **Review Excise Tax Obligations:** For businesses in industries subject to excise taxes, it is important to be aware of the specific tax rates, reporting requirements, and deadlines.

7. **Annual Reconciliation:** At the end of each year, reconcile your state and local tax filings with your financial statements. This will help you catch any discrepancies.

By following this checklist, you can stay organized, reduce the risk of errors, and maintain compliance with state and local tax laws.

Often Overlooked State and Local Taxes

While most businesses are familiar with common taxes like state income tax and sales tax, **there are several other state and local taxes that are commonly overlooked, which can lead to unexpected liabilities:**

1. **Local Business Licenses and Permits:** Depending on the city and county, businesses may be required to obtain and renew local business licenses and permits. These licenses are mandated by law and contribute to local government revenue. Neglecting to obtain or renew them can lead to penalties or, in severe cases, cause your business to shut down.

2. **Personal Property Tax:** Certain states and local governments levy taxes on the personal property of a business, including

machinery, equipment, and furniture. This tax is frequently overlooked because of its distinct nature from real estate property taxes.

3. **Franchise Taxes:** Certain states require businesses, especially corporations and LLCs, to pay franchise taxes for the privilege of doing business there. These taxes are often based on a company's net worth or gross receipts rather than its income. Be sure to verify if your business is subject to franchise taxes in any state where you operate.

4. **Special Assessments and Levies:** In some business areas, special assessments or levies, such as for infrastructure improvements or community development projects may be applicable. These are usually added to your property tax bill, or they are billed separately. Keep an eye out for any such assessments that may apply to your business.

By staying aware of these often-overlooked taxes, you can avoid unexpected costs and maintain full compliance with all state and local tax obligations.

Stay Ahead: Yearly Reviews and Updates

Tax laws and regulations can change frequently, and what was applicable in one year may not be applicable in the next. Therefore, setting aside time at the end of each fiscal year to review your business's tax filings, payments, and overall compliance with state and local tax requirements is important.

Start by revisiting your tax checklist and ensuring all necessary filings are completed accurately and on time. Next, review any changes in state and local tax laws that might affect your business. This includes updates to tax rates, new tax credits or deductions, and changes in filing requirements. Staying informed about these changes will allow you to adjust your tax strategy accordingly and take advantage of new opportunities to minimize taxes.

In addition, consider conducting an internal audit or working with a tax professional so that your records are accurate and up-to-date. Regular reviews will help you catch and correct any errors before they become costly problems and ensure that you're always prepared for potential audits.

The Golden Rule: When in Doubt, Ask

When it comes to state and local taxes, the complexity and variability of tax laws can leave many business owners feeling uncertain. The golden rule is one to follow: when in doubt, ask. Consulting with a tax professional can save you time, stress, and money by ensuring that you fully understand your tax obligations and are in compliance with all relevant local and state laws.

Tax professionals, such as CPAs or tax attorneys, have the expertise to understand the intricacies of state and local tax codes. They offer expertise on various aspects, from understanding filing requirements to maximizing available tax credits and deductions. Moreover, they can assist in pinpointing potential risks and creating strategies to address them.

If you're uncertain about any part of your state or local tax responsibilities, seeking professional guidance is highly advisable. It's an investment that can prevent costly mistakes and allow you a peace of mind, knowing your business is on solid ground.

Key Takeaways

- **Understand the Tax Landscape of Your State:** Each state has its unique tax requirements, making it crucial for businesses to stay informed.

- **Don't Ignore Local Taxes:** Beyond state taxes, local taxes like property, sales, and excise taxes can significantly impact your bottom line.

- **Employment Taxes Are a Dual Responsibility:** Compliance with both federal and state employment taxes is essential to avoid penalties.

- **Use a Checklist for Compliance:** A comprehensive checklist helps ensure that all state and local tax obligations are met.

- **Annual Reviews Are Crucial:** Regularly reviewing your tax obligations can prevent surprises and ensure your business stays compliant.

- **Seek Expert Advice:** When you're uncertain, consulting with tax professionals can help you avoid expensive errors.

CHAPTER 6

In the Trenches: Practical Steps to File Your Small Business Taxes

"Tax complexity itself is a kind of tax."
— **Max Baucus, Former U.S. Senator and Chairman of the Senate Finance Committee**

Filing Your Taxes in 7 Easy Steps

Step 1: Identifying the Right Tax Forms for Your Business

Your business type—whether it's a sole proprietorship, partnership, LLC, S corporation, or C corporation—determines which forms you need to file taxes correctly. For example, sole proprietors typically file using a Schedule C form along with their personal Form 1040, while partnerships file through Form 1065 and each partner uses a Schedule K-1. LLCs have the flexibility to file taxes as a sole proprietorship, partnership, or corporation, depending on the tax classification they select. S corporations report their income, deductions, and credits using Form 1120-S, which are then allocated to shareholders for their individual tax returns. In contrast, C corporations use Form 1120 and are liable for corporate income tax.

Accurately determining which tax forms apply to your business is crucial for staying compliant with IRS requirements and avoiding costly penalties. Using the wrong forms could result in either underpaying or overpaying taxes, both of which can lead to significant financial issues. To get started, consult the IRS website or a tax professional to confirm the forms required for your specific business structure.

Step 2: Compiling All Your Financial Data

Keeping your financial documents well-organized and easily accessible is essential for a hassle-free tax filing process. Begin by putting together your income statements, balance sheets, and cash flow reports, which together offer a comprehensive view of your business's financial health. These records are critical for accurately determining your gross income and total expenses.

Have detailed records prepared of all business expenses, including receipts, invoices, and bank statements, to support the deductions you intend to claim on your tax return. For businesses with employees, ensure that you have payroll records on hand to report wages, withholdings, and employment taxes correctly.

Consolidating all your financial information in one place can make the filing process more efficient and help minimize the risk of errors. Missing or incomplete records can lead to inaccurate tax filings, potentially resulting in audits or penalties.

Step 3: Claiming All Eligible Tax Deductions

Taking full advantage of tax deductions is a powerful strategy to reduce your taxable income and, consequently, your overall tax burden.

To make sure you're not missing out on any deductions, it's crucial to keep thorough records of your business expenditures throughout the year. To reiterate, if you use a portion of your home exclusively for business activities, you might be eligible for the home office deduction. Similarly, mileage for business-related travel can also be deducted, provided you keep a log of your business trips.

The Tax Cuts and Jobs Act (TCJA) introduced some changes to business deductions, such as a limitation applied to business meals and entertainment expense deductions. Stay informed of current tax laws and any potential changes that may affect your deductions. For example, the business meals deduction, which was temporarily expanded to 100% during the COVID-19 relief period, is expected to revert back to 50% if the TCJA provisions expire.

Step 4: Applying for All Applicable Tax Credits

There are several tax credits available for small businesses. **Review the table below and see which ones you may qualify for currently or can work towards qualifying for in the future:**

Tax Credit	Amount Credited	How to Qualify	How to File
Employee Retention Credit (ERC)	Up to $7,000 per employee per quarter (varies based on wages and eligibility)	Business operations affected by COVID-19 or experienced significant decline in gross receipts	Claim on Form 941 for eligible quarters; consult IRS guidelines
Earned Income Tax Credit (EITC)	Varies based on income, filing status, and number of dependents (up to $7,430 in 2023)	Must have earned income below a certain threshold; credit amount depends on income, filing status, and number of qualifying children	Claim on your personal tax return using IRS Form 1040 and Schedule EIC
Work Opportunity Tax Credit (WOTC)	Varies by employee group and wages (up to $9,600 per qualified employee)	Hire employees from targeted groups (e.g., veterans, ex-felons, individuals on government assistance)	File IRS Form 5884 after hiring eligible employees; certify via state workforce agency

Small Business Health Care Tax Credit	50% of employee health insurance premiums are paid for	Have fewer than 25 full-time equivalent employees, pay average wages below a certain threshold, and purchase insurance through SHOP	Purchase health insurance through the SHOP marketplace; file IRS Form 8941
Disabled Access Credit	50% of eligible expenses up to $10,250 annually	Offer paid family and medical leave to employees for at least two weeks annually	File IRS Form 8994 and include relevant employee wage details
Research and Development (R&D) Tax Credit	Up to 20% of eligible R&D expenses	Make energy-efficient improvements to commercial buildings, such as HVAC systems or lighting upgrades.	Calculate eligible deductions based on energy-efficient improvements and claim on IRS form 6765
Credit for Employer-Provided Childcare Facilities and Services	Up to 25% of childcare costs and 10% of resource expenses	Provide childcare facilities or contract childcare services for employees	File IRS Form 8882 for eligible childcare expenses

Researching available tax credits and consulting with a tax advisor can help you leverage these opportunities to significantly reduce the amount of tax you owe, freeing up more resources to invest back into your business.

Step 5: Calculating Your Total Tax Liability

Once you've identified the right tax forms, compiled your financial data, and claimed all eligible deductions and credits, the next step is to calculate your total tax liability. This process involves determining how much tax you owe after taking into account your taxable income, deductions, and credits.

Begin by determining your taxable income. This is calculated by subtracting deductions from your total income. For instance, if your business generated $100,000 in revenue and your deductions amount to $30,000, your taxable income would be $70,000. Next, apply the appropriate tax rates to your taxable income. Depending on your business structure i.e. whether you're a sole proprietor, partnership, corporation, or an S Corporation, your tax rate will be determined accordingly. .

Based on your taxable income and tax rate, you can calculate the preliminary tax liability and then subtract any tax credits that your business is eligible for.

To avoid errors, use tax software or consult a tax professional to make sure calculations are correct and accurate by ensuring that you've applied the correct rates and credits. This will double-check that you only pay the amount of tax you owe and avoid any underpayment penalties.

Step 6: Reviewing and Finalizing Your Tax Return

Before you file your tax return, it's important to carefully review it to confirm that all information is correct, and nothing has been overlooked. Errors on your tax return can lead to processing delays, penalties, or even an audit, so take your time to check the work carefully.

Begin by reviewing all entries for accuracy, including your income, deductions, credits, and any other figures reported on your tax forms. Ensure all calculations are correct and that you've applied the appropriate tax rates. Double-check that you've included all necessary forms and schedules, especially if your business operates across multiple states or has various sources of income.

It's also important to verify that you've included all required documentation to back your submission, such as receipts, invoices, and any other important records. The supporting documents need not be submitted with your return, but they should be readily available in case of an audit.

Another key aspect of finalizing your return is ensuring that all personal and business information is accurate. If you make mistakes in your name, address, or taxpayer identification number, you may suffer consequences such as processing issues and delays. If you're e-filing, confirm that the IRS and state tax authorities have accepted your return. If you're mailing your return, use a service that provides delivery confirmation.

Step 7: Your Tax Return - Filing on Time

Filing your tax return by the deadline is essential to prevent penalties and interest, which can add up quickly. The IRS imposes a penalty for late filings, typically 5% of the unpaid tax amount per month, but the rate may go up to a maximum of 25%. Moreover, if you owe taxes and miss the payment deadline, you'll face an additional penalty and interest on the outstanding balance.

For most small businesses, the tax filing deadline coincides with the individual tax deadline, typically April 15th. However, certain business structures, like partnerships and S Corporations, have earlier deadlines, usually mid-March. Note the specific deadline that applies to your business so that you may plan your filings and work accordingly.

If you're unable to finalize your tax return by the deadline, filing for an extension is a wise option. The IRS grants an automatic six-month extension, extending your filing deadline to October 15th. However, it's important to note that this extension applies only to filing, not to payment—any taxes owed are still due by the original deadline, and interest will be charged on any unpaid amounts.

To request for an extension, you must file the IRS Form 4868 online or by mail. Most tax preparation software also offers a simple way to request for an extension with minimal effort. Even if you file for an extension, it is best to try to estimate your tax liability as accurately as possible and make a payment to reduce any potential penalties and interest.

Troubleshooting Common Filing Issues

Dealing with Missing or Incomplete Records

Dealing with missing or incomplete records can be one of the most challenging aspects of filing taxes for your small business. Accurate and comprehensive records are the backbone of successfully filing your taxes, and without them, you risk underreporting income, missing out on deductions, or triggering an audit. However, even with the best intentions, sometimes records go missing, or you realize that your bookkeeping wasn't as thorough as it should have been.

The first step in handling missing or incomplete records is to gather as much information as possible from alternative sources. Bank statements, credit card records, and even emails can help you piece together the details of transactions. For example, if you're missing receipts for certain expenses, your bank or credit card statement may be adequate proof for tax purposes, especially if the transactions are business-related.

It's always best to err on the side of caution. So, if you can't find specific records, consider estimating the amounts based on available and authentic information. It's better to under-claim a deduction than to overestimate it and risk penalties. Thoroughly document your estimation process, ensuring it reflects the most accurate information available at the time. This documentation can be crucial if the IRS questions your calculations.

If you're unable to recreate the necessary records, it may be wise to consult with a professional for assistance. An accountant or tax professional can guide you on the best course of action, including potential steps for making adjustments or amending previous filings. They can also help you establish better record-keeping practices moving forward to avoid similar issues in the future.

The key to dealing with missing records is to stay proactive. Take immediate steps to address the gaps, document your efforts, and seek professional advice when necessary.

Dual State Taxes for Multistate Businesses

It can be a challenge to sort through dual state taxes, particularly for businesses operating in multiple states. Each state has its own set of tax laws. Businesses must comply with the tax obligations in every state where they are physically present, generate significant income, or have employees. This includes but is not limited to: state income, sales, and franchise tax.Determining your nexus in each state is the first step in managing dual state taxes. Nexus is the legal term that describes the level of connection that your business has with a state, which obligates you to pay taxes there. Factors that can establish nexus include the presence of a physical location for business, employees, inventory, or significant sales in the state.

Once you've established nexus, you must file the appropriate tax returns in each state that meets the requirements. This can be tricky, as each state may have different filing requirements, deadlines, and tax rates. To manage this process effectively, consider using tax software designed for multistate businesses, which can help you keep track of various obligations and ensure accurate filings.

It's also important to consult with a tax professional who is knowledgeable about multistate taxation. They can provide guidance on how to minimize your tax liability across different states, ensure compliance with varying regulations, and avoid double taxation.

Correcting Mistakes on Submitted Returns

When you submit tax returns, there are chances of mistakes. It is important to correct them right away to avoid potential penalties or interest. The process for amending a tax return is straightforward and involves filing Form 1040-X, the Amended U.S. Individual Income Tax Return. This form allows you to correct errors, such as misreported income, overlooked deductions, or incorrect filing status.

When filling out Form 1040-X, you'll need to explain the reason for the amendment and provide corrected figures. It is necessary to include any additional forms for the amendment or schedules affected by the changes. For example, if you're correcting a business deduction, you'll need to include an updated Schedule C.

After submitting the amended return, it's wise to keep thorough records of the changes and any correspondence with the IRS. If you discover an error on your return, acting fast can minimize potential complications. Remember, you generally have up to three years from the original filing deadline, or two years from the date you paid the tax—whichever comes later—to submit an amended return.

Responding to an Audit Notice

Receiving an IRS audit notice is scary, but responding calmly is crucial. An audit doesn't necessarily mean that there's a problem; it could simply be that your return was selected for further review. First, carefully read the audit notice to acknowledge what the IRS is questioning and what they are requesting for, in terms of forms or documents.

Once you understand the focus of the audit, gather all the relevant records and documentation. For example, if the audit concerns specific deductions, have all receipts, invoices, and other evidence supporting your claims ready. When replying to the IRS, be brief and supply only the information they have asked for—avoiding unnecessary details that could complicate matters.

Resolving Payment Issues and Back Taxes

If you're struggling to pay your tax bill or have accumulated back taxes, it's important to address the issue proactively. Ignoring payment problems can mean interest charges or even penalties, possibly legal action from the IRS. Start by reviewing your tax bill to ensure it's accurate, then explore your payment options.

The IRS offers several solutions for taxpayers facing payment difficulties. One option is setting up an installment agreement, enabling you to pay your tax debt with smaller installments. If your financial situation is severe, you may be eligible for an 'Offer in Compromise', where the IRS agrees to settle your debt for less than the total amount owed.

It's important to reach out to the IRS promptly if you're unable to pay your taxes in full. By taking the initiative, you can often negotiate a payment plan or other resolution that prevents more severe consequences.

Examples of How Small Businesses Handle Tax Filing

Jane's Sole Proprietor's Journey Through Tax Season

Jane, a freelance graphic designer, operates as a sole proprietor, which means her business income is reported directly on her personal tax return using Schedule C. As tax season approached, Jane faced the challenge of organizing her financial records, which included tracking numerous small business expenses like software subscriptions, client lunches, and travel costs. To streamline the process, she used accounting software to categorize her expenses and generate detailed reports.

One of the key challenges Jane encountered was accurately calculating her self-employment taxes, which included both Social Security and Medicare contributions. Working with a tax advisor ensured that all her deductions were correctly applied, reducing her taxable income.

How a Home-Based Business Mastered Tax Filing

Tom, who runs a successful home-based e-commerce business, faced unique tax challenges due to his use of a dedicated home office. Understanding that the home office deduction could significantly lower his taxable income, Tom tracked his home office expenses, including a portion of his rent, utilities, and internet costs.

He also kept detailed records of inventory purchases, shipping costs, and other business-related expenses, using digital tools to organize receipts and invoices. During tax season, Tom was able to maximize his deductions by accurately calculating the percentage of his home used for business and applying it to his overall home expenses.

How a Family Business Overcame Inheritance Tax Issues

The Thompson family, owners of a third-generation family bakery, faced significant inheritance tax challenges when the business was passed down from the founders to the next generation. The inheritance tax liability was substantial with the bakery's assets, including valuable real estate and equipment. To navigate this complex situation, the Thompsons sought the expertise of a tax attorney who specialized in estate planning and business succession.

The family worked closely with their attorney to structure the transfer of ownership to minimize the tax burden. They utilized strategies such as gifting portions of the business over time to reduce the estate's taxable value and took advantage of any available exemptions. Additionally, the attorney helped them establish a family trust, which provided further protection against future tax liabilities.

Key Takeaways

1. **Identify and Use the Right Tax Forms:** Ensure that you're using the correct tax forms based on your business structure to avoid errors and delays.

2. **Keep Comprehensive Financial Records:** Properly compile all financial data before filing to streamline the tax process.

3. **Make the Most of Deductions and Credits:** Fully utilize all eligible deductions and credits to significantly lower your tax liability.

4. **Double-Check Your Return for Accuracy:** Carefully review your tax return before you submit it to prevent costly errors.

5. **Troubleshoot Common Issues:** Be prepared to handle common filing issues, such as dealing with incomplete records or responding to an audit.

6. **Learn from Real-Life Examples:** Real-world case studies offer valuable insights into handling tax challenges successfully.

CHAPTER 7

Loopholes, Deductions, and Legal Magic: Maximizing Tax Savings

"The art of taxation consists in so plucking the goose as to obtain the largest possible amount of feathers with the smallest possible amount of hissing."
— **Jean-Baptiste Colbert, French Minister of Finances under King Louis XIV.**

Minimizing State and Local Taxes, Including Sales Tax

State Tax Savings

State taxes can vary significantly depending on where your business is located. For example, certain states offer tax incentives for hiring workers in specific regions, investing in sustainable energy, or engaging in research and development activities. Additionally, many states offer incentives for businesses that relocate to or expand within their borders, including tax abatements and reductions on property taxes.

To take advantage of these opportunities, it's a good idea to stay informed about the specific tax benefits available in your state. Keeping a tab on your state's Department of Revenue's website or seeking advice from a local tax expert may prove helpful in uncovering and claiming available tax incentives. You can effectively lower your overall tax burden by aligning your business strategies and investments with the tax benefits offered by the states

State Specific Incentives

Some state specific incentives will help you understand the types of opportunities you should be familiar with. For instance, New York's 'Excelsior Jobs Program' offers tax credits to businesses that create jobs or make significant capital investments within the state. Companies in industries like biotechnology, software development, and manufacturing can qualify for these credits, which can include reductions in corporate income taxes and property tax exemptions. Your business has to meet specific job creation or investment thresholds and apply through New York's Empire State Development agency. The goal is to incentivize businesses to invest in high-growth sectors and expand within the state.

California's Enterprise Zone Program provides tax benefits to businesses located in designated geographic areas targeted for economic revitalization. These benefits include hiring credits, sales tax credits, and a reduction in the taxes for purchasing equipment or investing in local infrastructure. To qualify for these incentives, businesses must be located within an enterprise zone, such as certain areas of Los Angeles or Fresno. In addition, compliance with certain hiring requirement policies, such as hiring disadvantaged workers on a regular basis can also make your business an eligible candidate.

Local governments also offer tax reductions and rebates to encourage economic development. For example, cities like Austin, Texas, provide payroll tax credits to businesses that create a specific number of jobs or build new facilities for local people. These local incentives often complement state programs, creating a multi-layered tax strategy that businesses can avail to their benefit.

Minimizing Local Taxes

Local taxes, such as city or county taxes, can also impact your business's bottom line. These taxes often include local income taxes, business licenses, and special district taxes that fund specific services like transportation or sanitation. For example, some cities offer tax breaks for businesses that operate within designated enterprise zones, which are areas targeted for economic revitalization.

Additionally, local governments may provide reductions on business license fees or offer rebates for businesses that contribute to community development projects. Engaging with local economic development agencies can help you discover these opportunities and reduce your local tax obligations.

Sales Taxes: Collecting from Customers

Sales tax compliance is critical to operating a business that sells goods or services. Neglecting to comply can lead to penalties and interest charges. To stay compliant, businesses need to keep up with the sales tax rates in the areas where they operate and sell.

Moreover, adopting sales tax automation software can simplify the process. These tools automatically calculate accurate tax rates based on the customer's location, minimizing the chances of errors.

Property Tax: Real Estate Realities

Property taxes are a significant expense for businesses that own real estate and vary widely based on the location. Understanding how property taxes are assessed and knowing your rights to appeal assessments can lead to substantial savings. In some cases, businesses may be eligible for property tax exemptions or reductions based on the nature of their operations or improvements made to the property.

Regularly reviewing your property tax assessments and considering professional appraisals can help avoid overpaying. Additionally, considering the local tax environment and being strategic about where you purchase, or lease property can further reduce your property tax burden.

Property Tax Reassessments

There are certain strategies that help to reduce property taxes through property tax reassessments. For example, if you think your property has been overvalued, you can appeal the assessment. This process typically involves gathering evidence, such as recent sale prices of similar properties in the area or demonstrating that the property has depreciated due to age or other factors.

In urban settings, such as downtown office spaces, reassessment appeals can be useful when property values fluctuate dramatically due to changes in the commercial real estate market. Property tax assessments should regularly be reviewed, and professional advice should be considered if business owners wish to make an appeal. This is especially when significant upgrades, zoning changes, or market shifts occur that could impact property values. Successfully lowering property tax assessments can lead to long-term savings.

Don't Miss Any Potential Tax Savings

Common Small Business Loopholes

Maximizing Retirement Plans for Tax Deferral

Retirement plans offer tax-saving opportunities for small business owners. The key lies in selecting the best plan that will most impact the level of tax deferral. For instance, a Solo 401(k) can be an excellent tool for high-income earners because it allows business owners to defer more income than a SEP IRA. The Solo 401(k) offers both employee and employer contribution options, allowing for higher contributions if the business owner earns a substantial income. In 2024, the combined contribution limit for a Solo 401(k) is $69,000, plus a catch-up contribution for those over the age of 50. The SEP IRA, on the other hand, only allows employer contributions capped at 25% of salary or $69,000, whichever is less.

The Hidden Benefits of Health Savings Accounts (HSAs)

Health Savings Accounts (HSAs) are another useful tool that small business owners can leverage in the long run. While contributions to HSAs are tax-deductible and grow tax-free, a lesser-known benefit is that they can also be used for tax-free withdrawals for medical expenses at the time of retirement. Since HSA funds roll over year to year, you could build a large balance that can be used later in life to cover medical costs, effectively turning the HSA into a retirement health fund. An HSA creates a triple-benefit opportunity for business owners: deductible contributions, tax-free growth, and tax-free withdrawals for qualified expenses.

Avoiding IRS Scrutiny with the S-Corp Salary-Dividend Split

The S-Corporation salary-dividend split is another common tax-saving strategy. S-Corp owners can pay themselves a reasonable salary, which is subject to employment taxes, while distributing the remaining profits as dividends, which are not subject to self-employment taxes. However, many small business owners misuse this strategy by paying themselves an unreasonably low salary to avoid payroll taxes, which can trigger IRS scrutiny and penalties. It's important to maintain a balance between a reasonable salary and high dividends. Consulting with a tax professional in this matter can help.

Deductions: A Beat-by-Beat Breakdown of Expense Claims

Maximizing Travel Expense Deductions

Travel expenses are one of the most frequently applied deductions small business owners are entitled to claim. Deductible travel costs include airfare, hotel accommodations, car rentals, and meals paid for, while traveling for business purposes. For example, if a business owner attends an out-of-state industry conference, all associated travel costs are deductible, as long as they are properly documented. Don't forget to keep everything related to the expenses - including receipts and a log detailing the business purpose of the trip, as the IRS may request proof.

Employee Benefits as Deductions

Employee benefits are another type of deduction, which is often underutilized. Health insurance premiums, retirement plan contributions, and even education reimbursement for employees are all costs that can be deducted from the business's taxable income. One thing many companies do to attract and retain top talent is to offer benefits to their employees, which are also tax deductible, thus lowering the tax liability.

The Home Office Deduction

For entrepreneurs managing remote businesses, home office deductions can be availed to reduce business tax owed. A portion of household expenses—such as rent, utilities, and home maintenance expenses—can be deducted if the home office is regularly used for business purposes. The IRS offers a choice of two methods for calculating the home office deduction: the simplified method, which allows a standard deduction of $5 per square foot of office space, or the actual expense method, which involves deducting a percentage of the costs associated with maintaining the home office.

The Tax Cuts and Jobs Act (TCJA) introduced substantial changes to deductions, most notably by introducing 100% bonus depreciation. This provision allows businesses to immediately deduct the full cost of qualifying assets purchased between September 27, 2017, and January 1, 2023. However, the bonus depreciation benefit is set to phase out gradually. Starting in 2023, the deduction decreases by 20% per year, meaning that by 2025, businesses can only deduct 60% of the asset cost in the year of purchase. This phase-out will continue until bonus depreciation is fully eliminated by 2027.

Credits: Earning Back Money

Tax credits offer a powerful way for small businesses to lower their tax bills by directly reducing the amount owed to the IRS, in contrast to simply decreasing taxable income in the way that deductions do. A proper understanding and utilization of these credits can allow for substantial tax savings. You can refer to the table in chapter six for a comprehensive list of available credits. Keep in mind that all credit options available are not covered in the table, just some of the most common ones. So, be sure to do your own research as well.

An important consideration for the Research and Development (R&D) Tax Credit is that businesses must meet the IRS's four-part test to qualify. This includes proving that the research is technological in nature, aimed at eliminating uncertainty, and involves a process of experimentation. The credit is calculated as a percentage of qualifying research expenses, which may include wages for employees engaged in R&D, supplies, and contract research costs. To claim this credit, businesses can use IRS Form 6765. To maximize credits, it is essential to maintain detailed records of eligible activities and expenses throughout the year.

Case Studies: Small Businesses That Maximized Tax Savings

How ABC Enterprises Lowered Its Liability Through Deductions

ABC Enterprises, a small manufacturing company, significantly reduced its tax liability by strategically leveraging deductions available under Section 179 and the Tax Cuts and Jobs Act (TCJA). By investing in new machinery, the business was able to deduct the full purchase price of the machinery, providing immediate tax relief. Additionally, TCJA's bonus depreciation clause allowed 100% depreciation on qualified property at that time, which ABC Enterprises took full advantage of. This combination of deductions enabled ABC Enterprises to reduce its taxable income by a substantial amount, allowing the company to reinvest the savings towards further expansion. As a result, the business grew its operations by continuously upgrading its manufacturing capabilities without bearing a significant tax burden allowing it to gain a competitive edge in the market.e

Jane's Sole Proprietorship Case: Claiming Credits

Jane, a sole proprietor running a small graphic design business, maximized her tax savings by thoroughly researching and claiming all available tax credit opportunities. By taking advantage of the Earned Income Tax Credit (EITC), intended for low-to-moderate-income earners, Jane was able to substantially lower her overall tax bill. Additionally, she claimed credits for education expenses to cover the cost of a specialized design course she took to enhance her skills. These credits, combined with careful planning and diligent record-keeping, allowed Jane to minimize her tax bill while continuing to invest in her professional development.

Key Takeaways

- **State and Local Tax Planning:** Understanding and navigating state and local tax laws can lead to significant savings, particularly through credits, deductions, and strategic location choices.

- **Leveraging Legal Loopholes:** Small businesses can reduce their tax burden by legally exploiting available loopholes in the tax system, including setting up retirement plans, health savings accounts, and selecting an appropriate business structure.

- **Maximizing Deductions:** The TCJA has introduced significant changes that lead to more deduction opportunities, such as bonus depreciation, which businesses can use to lower their tax obligations.

- **Utilizing Tax Credits:** Tax credits directly reduce the amount of tax owed and can be a game-changer for small businesses. Businesses should explore credit options like WOTC and R&D to maximize their savings.

- **Learning from Real-Life Success Stories:** Case studies of small businesses demonstrate the practical application of tax-saving strategies, highlighting the importance of proactive tax planning.

- **Staying Informed:** The tax landscape is constantly evolving, and small business owners must stay updated on changes like the phase-out options of bonus depreciation to continue maximizing their tax savings.

Chapter 8

Help Is at Hand: Using CPAs and Small Business Tax Services

"The income tax has made more liars out of the American people than golf has."
— **Will Rogers, American humorist and social commentator**

When to Seek Professional Help

Identifying Red Flags

As your business grows, so will the time you spend managing its financial and tax responsibilities. It's important to recognize when these tasks are getting out of hand, as addressing issues early can save you from costly errors and stress. Professional tax assistance might be necessary if you encounter certain warning signs. **Here are key indicators that suggest when it might be time to consult with a tax expert:**

1. **Frequent Errors in Filings:** Consistent mistakes, such as misclassified income or overlooked deductions, can lead to IRS penalties and audits. Professional help can prevent these.

2. **IRS Notices:** Unexpected IRS letters often indicate underlying issues. A tax professional can help you address these notices promptly and correctly.

3. **Difficulty Keeping Up with Tax Laws:** If staying updated on tax regulations feels overwhelming or you're unsure of how recent changes may impact your business, a professional can ensure compliance.

4. **Complex Financial Records:** Managing your financial records can become more challenging as your business expands. If reconciling accounts takes too long, an accountant can streamline this process.

5. **Stressful Tax Preparation:** If tax preparation has become very time-consuming or stressful, it is an indication that your tax situation is too complex to handle alone.

6. **Uncertainty About Deductions and Credits:** Not confident that you're maximizing deductions and credits? A tax professional can help you claim all eligible benefits, reducing your tax liability.

When Taxes Feel Like a Jungle

Figuring out tax regulations can feel like a journey through a dense jungle, where you're trying to figure your way out. The U.S. tax code is notoriously complex, with rules changing every year or even mid-year. This complexity can be overwhelming for small business owners, leading to missed deadlines, overlooked deductions, and the chance of occurring penalties. The challenge isn't just about filing taxes correctly; it's also about understanding tax credits, deductions, and regulations that apply to your specific business. The pressure of staying compliant while also running a business can cause significant stress and anxiety. When you start feeling lost in the details or are uncertain about how to process your taxes, it's a clear sign that professional guidance could save you time, money, and a lot of headaches.

When Your Tax Debts are Sinking Your Ship

Accumulating significant tax debt can feel like a heavy anchor dragging your business down, threatening its financial stability and future growth. Accruing penalties and interest are some of the risks associated with tax debt accumulation. It can quickly balloon the amount you owe. If left unaddressed, these debts could lead to liens on your business assets, garnished wages, or even the forced sale of your property. It's important to seek professional help as soon as you realize your tax debts are becoming difficult to manage. A qualified CPA or tax attorney can assist in negotiating repayment plans with the IRS, exploring settlement options through offers in compromise, or advising on whether bankruptcy might be a wise option.

Tax Planning for Businesses Approaching $1 Million in Revenue

As a business grows and hits bigger numbers in revenue, like its first million dollars, tax planning becomes even more crucial. By engaging professional tax advisors at this stage, your business can optimize its deductions and credits, creating an efficient business tax structure. In addition, they can assist in the creation of a strategy to reinvest profits, manage payroll taxes, and prepare for potential audit triggers.

Transitioning from Sole Proprietorship to LLC

Many small businesses start as sole proprietorships due to the simplicity of the business structure, but as the business grows, transitioning to an LLC or another type of entity can offer better legal protection and tax advantages. This requires careful planning, particularly regarding taxes. A CPA or tax attorney can guide the business owner through the legal process of forming an LLC, handling the associated tax implications, and maximizing deductions and tax benefits.

For example, an independent contractor who has been operating as a sole proprietor might need help in setting up an LLC to limit their personal liability, while also changing their tax filing from Schedule C to a different form, depending on the type of LLC.

International Expansion

For businesses planning to expand internationally, whether by selling products overseas or setting up offices across different countries, taxes become way more complex. International tax treaties, VAT (value-added tax), and differing tax regulations require careful navigation. A tax professional experienced in international business can provide the necessary expertise to ensure compliance with foreign tax laws while optimizing the U.S. tax impact. For instance, a U.S.-based, tech company expanding its operations into Europe, must understand the complexities of VAT, local corporate tax rates, and transfer pricing regulations. A CPA specializing in international tax can create a plan that accounts for these factors while minimizing global tax liabilities.

Other Reasons You May Need a Pro

There are several other scenarios where opting for professional tax assistance could prove invaluable:

- If your business expands to new markets, whether across states or internationally, it comes with new tax obligations that can be difficult to navigate without expert advice.

- Your business is selected for an audit.

- Significant changes take place in your business such as a merger, acquisition, or restructuring.

- The structure of your business changes

- Your business owns significant assets, so you require estate planning to ensure that they are passed on in the most tax-efficient manner possible.

Choosing a Reliable CPA or Tax Accountant

Investigating Potential Providers

In your search for the best CPA or tax accountant, thorough research is required to find a professional who can meet your business's specific needs. Start by checking the qualifications of potential providers, ensuring they are certified and have the necessary licenses to practice in your state. Experience plays an important role too. Look for a CPA who is working with businesses in your industry or facing similar financial complexities, with a proven track record. Additionally, client reviews and testimonials can provide insights into a provider's reliability, communication skills, and ability to deliver results. Don't hesitate to ask for references from current or past clients to gain firsthand accounts of their experiences. Also, verify that the CPA stays current with tax laws and regulations, as these can change frequently and impact your business.

Finding a CPA Near You

Professional directories, such as those provided by the American Institute of Certified Public Accountants (AICPA), can be valuable tools for finding licensed CPAs that meet your set criteria. These directories often include filters for narrowing down candidates based on specialization, location, and other relevant factors, making it easier to find a CPA who aligns with your needs.

Personal recommendations from other business owners, colleagues, or members of your local business network can also help you find trusted professionals with proven track records. Word of mouth remains one of the most reliable ways to discover a competent CPA because it's based on firsthand experiences. When seeking recommendations, inquire about the CPA's responsiveness, expertise, and ability to resolve cumbersome tax issues.

Online platforms like LinkedIn are another useful tool to search for CPAs in your area. LinkedIn allows you to review a CPA's professional background, endorsements, and connections. Many profiles include client testimonials and details on specific areas of expertise.

Don't overlook local business associations or chambers of commerce, which often have lists of recommended service providers, including CPAs. These organizations typically vet their members, which adds an additional layer of trust. Attending local business events or networking meetups hosted by these organizations can also give you the opportunity to meet potential CPAs in person and assess if they would be a good fit for your business.

Consider creating a shortlist of potential CPAs and scheduling consultations with each for a more comprehensive approach. During these meetings, discuss your business needs, ask about their experiences with businesses similar to yours, and evaluate how well they communicate and understand your specific concerns.

Recognizing Iffy Tax Service Providers

When selecting a tax service provider, look for red flags that indicate unreliability or unethical practices. An example of a significant warning sign is a provider who guarantees large refunds before even reviewing your financial information—this is misleading and suggests that they may be using aggressive or questionable tactics that could put you at risk. Overpromising is a tactic that unscrupulous providers use to lure in clients, but it can lead to serious legal consequences if those promises are based on unethical practices.

Another red flag is the lack of proper credentials. Always verify that the provider is a certified professional, such as a CPA or an enrolled agent, with the appropriate licenses to practice in your state. A provider who cannot show proof of certification or dismisses the importance of credentials may lack the necessary expertise to handle your taxes correctly. In some cases, these individuals may even be participating in illegal operations which could leave you vulnerable if issues arise with your tax filings.

Additionally, be cautious of providers who are reluctant to provide references or have negative reviews online. Transparency is key; if a provider is unwilling to discuss their methods or explain how they arrived at certain figures, it's best to look elsewhere.

Another warning sign is a provider who pressures you to sign blank tax forms, or who wants to deposit your refund into their account before forwarding it to you. These practices can be indicative of fraud, and you could be held accountable for any false information submitted on your behalf.

Finally, consider the location and accessibility of the provider. A tax service that solely operates online or does not have a support team that can easily be reached, may leave you without recourse in case of disputes or problems with your return.

Additional Red Flags to Watch Out For

Here are some additional key indicators to watch out for:

1. **Excessive Fees for Basic Filings:** If a tax service provider charges high fees for simple returns or common business filings, it's a clear red flag. Some providers take advantage of small business owners who may not be aware of standard pricing for tax services. Compare rates with industry averages and seek transparency in billing practices. Always ask for a detailed breakdown of what the fees cover before agreeing to any services.

2. **Aggressive Tactics that Risk Audits:** A common red flag is when a provider guarantees large refunds without thoroughly reviewing your financial records or by suggesting risky deductions

that may trigger an audit. While it's important to maximize deductions, these must always comply with IRS guidelines. If a provider is too aggressive or promises results that seem too good to be true, they probably are, and you could end up facing hefty penalties down the line.

3. **Unresponsiveness During Critical Times:** Tax service providers who are difficult to reach, especially during tax season, pose a significant risk to your business. A provider's lack of responsiveness at the time of filing deadlines or when dealing with IRS correspondence can lead to these deadlines being missed, your business being subjected to penalties, or tax issues left unaddressed. Choose a provider with a strong reputation for clear communication and accessibility during busy periods.

4. **Pressuring Clients to Sign Blank Forms:** If a tax preparer asks you to sign blank forms or sign off on documents without letting you review them, this is a major red flag. This unethical practice can result in fraudulent tax filings under your name, which could have legal consequences. Always review all tax documents before signing them and ensure that every figure and statement is accurate.

5. **Lack of Proper Credentials:** Verify that the tax professional has the necessary credentials for the job, such as a CPA qualification or they are an enrolled agent. Tax preparers who are not certified may not have the expertise required to handle complex business tax filings, and their lack of credentials could leave you vulnerable if there are errors or discrepancies.

Common Scams and How to Avoid Them

1. **Refund Fraud:** This scam involves a tax preparer submitting false information on your behalf to inflate your tax refund. After receiving the refund, they take their cut, leaving you liable for

repaying the IRS once the fraud is detected. To avoid this, always review your return in detail, ask questions about any unfamiliar deductions, and confirm that the refund amount seems reasonable based on your actual financial situation.

2. **Phishing for Personal Information:** Some tax service providers may attempt to gather personal information such as your Social Security Number or bank account details with the intent to commit identity theft. Be cautious about who you share sensitive data with. Always work with trusted, credentialed professionals who prioritize data security.

Choosing a CPA Who'll Fight for You

Selecting a CPA who is competent and dedicated to your business's success can have a significant impact. on how your business's finances are managed. A proactive CPA will go beyond simply preparing your tax returns—they will stay ahead of changes in tax laws, regularly review your financials, and offer strategic advice to help you minimize tax liabilities and maximize savings. Look for a CPA who is communicative and easy to reach, someone who keeps you informed and explains perplexing tax issues in a way that you can understand. They should also be detail-oriented, meticulously ensuring that every deduction and credit is claimed accurately and legally.

A CPA, who is truly on your side, will be an advocate for your business, particularly if you face an audit or other tax-related challenges. They will represent your interests in front of the IRS, ensuring that you are treated fairly and that any disputes are resolved in your favor.

Making the Most of Your Tax Accountant's Skills and Knowledge

Getting Every Penny's Worth from Your CPA

To maximize the value of your CPA's services, it's necessary to collaborate with them, instead of just handing over your financial documents. Start by aligning expectations with each other—communicate your business goals, tax planning needs, and any specific areas where you need their expertise. An indication of a strong partnership is regular communication with things like scheduled periodic check-ins to discuss your financial status, upcoming tax deadlines, and any changes in tax laws that might affect your business. You should also get a sense of whether their take on tax laws is more aggressive or conservative. Aggressiveness can help you save money, but you should be prepared for the potential risks it may entail. A more conservative approach means that you'll likely end up paying more upfront, but it allows you to gain peace of mind. Another important aspect is reviewing the work your CPA shares with you. While they are the experts, you should still review the reports, tax returns, and financial statements they prepare. Ask questions when something is unclear and ensure that all deductions and credits applicable to your business have been correctly applied.

Additionally, be proactive in providing your CPA with complete and accurate information. The more detailed and organized your records are, the more effective the CPA's attempt will be to minimize your tax liability and improve your financial health.

Building a Relationship with Your CPA

Building a long-term, trust-based relationship with your CPA can be significantly beneficial for your business. When your CPA is familiar with your financial history, business model, and personal goals, they can provide more personalized advice and improve strategic planning for your business. This ongoing relationship allows your CPA to identify trends and patterns in your finances, helping you anticipate challenges and seize opportunities for growth.

Decoding Tax Language with Your CPA's Help

Tax law is notoriously strenuous, filled with jargon and legalese that can be difficult for business owners to comprehend. This is where your CPA becomes valuable in managing your taxes and translating difficult tax language into a version that you can understand. When your CPA takes the time to explain the intricacies of tax codes, deductions, and credits, it empowers you to make informed decisions about your business's finances.

Don't hesitate to ask your CPA to break down difficult concepts or clarify any aspects of your tax return that seem confusing. A well-qualified CPA will ensure that you fully understand their recommended tax strategies, along with their financial implications.

Examples of Businesses That Benefit from Professional Tax Services

Cinderella: From Tax Troubles to Happy Ever After

Once upon a time, a small family-owned bakery found itself raveled in a tax nightmare. The business, which had grown rapidly in recent years, was facing mounting tax debts and IRS penalties due to a combination of missed filings and incomplete records. The owners, overwhelmed and unsure of how to resolve the situation, sought the help of a seasoned CPA.

The CPA immediately took charge, organizing the bakery's financial records and correcting past filing errors. They negotiated with the IRS on the bakery's behalf, successfully reducing the penalties and setting up a manageable payment plan for the outstanding tax debt. However, the CPA's work did not stop there. They implemented a tax strategy that helped the bakery take full advantage of deductions and credits, previously gone unnoticed.

Within a year, the bakery resolved its tax issues and witnessed improved cash flow and financial stability. Once burdened by stress and uncertainty, the owners were now free to focus on growing their business. With the CPA's continued guidance, the bakery's story transformed from tax troubles to financial success.

The Lion King Legacy: Building a Financial Kingdom with Tax Savings

A luxury real estate firm, known for its high-end properties, was looking to build a strong financial foundation to support its long-term growth plan. While the firm was profitable, its founders knew they were not fully capitalizing on potential tax savings. They decided to bring in a top-tier CPA firm with experience in real estate to help them.

The CPA firm conducted an in-depth analysis of the real estate company's finances and identified several tax saving opportunities. They implemented a series of strategies, including the usage of cost segregation studies to accelerate depreciation on the company's properties, reducing its taxable income significantly. The CPA also helped the firm take advantage of energy efficiency credits and other incentives designed for the real estate industry.

As a result, the real estate firm was able to save millions in taxes over the next few years. These savings were reinvested into the business, funding new projects and expanding their portfolio.

Key Takeaways

- **Know When to Seek Help:** Understanding when your business tax situation requires professional expertise to prevent costly mistakes and ensure compliance with tax laws.

- **Choose Wisely:** Selecting the right CPA or tax accountant is crucial—look for experience, trustworthiness, and a commitment to your business's financial success.

- **Build the Relationship:** Collaborating closely with your tax professional can enhance your financial planning strategy and maximize your tax savings.

- **Understand Tax Language:** A good CPA will help you understand difficult tax terms to help you make informed business decisions.

- **Real-Life Success:** Case studies highlight how businesses have overcome tax challenges and achieved financial stability through professional help.

- **Leverage Expertise for Growth:** Professional tax services not only help in compliance but also provide opportunities for tax savings that can be reinvested into your business.

CHAPTER 9

The More You Know: Staying Current & Resources for Small Businesses

"Ignorance of the law excuses no one."
— **Legal Maxim**

Keeping Informed on the Constantly Evolving Tax Code

Understanding the Rhythm of Tax Law Changes

Tax laws are constantly evolving, with federal, state, and local governments frequently updating regulations to reflect changes in the economy, political priorities, and societal needs. These adjustments can range from small updates, like changes in tax rates or deductions, to sweeping overhauls, such as the introduction of the Tax Cuts and Jobs Act (TCJA) of 2017.

Tax laws are typically reviewed annually at the federal level, with Congress sometimes passing new legislation that can significantly impact small businesses. Meanwhile, state and local governments may adjust tax policies more frequently, depending on their unique economic circumstances. A missed update by the business owner could result in the overpayment of taxes or failure to comply with new rules, potentially leading to penalties.

The Importance of Yearly Tax Updates

Yearly tax updates are required to stay current with the latest IRS rules, regulations, and tax code adjustments. These updates can directly impact how businesses file taxes, claim deductions, or calculate their tax liability.

The IRS releases yearly bulletins and guidelines that outline new regulations and provide detailed explanations for tax filing processes. For small businesses, these updates can include changes to allowable deductions, credits, filing deadlines, and new tax forms. For example, adjustments to the standard mileage rate or updates to employee tax withholding tables may affect how businesses track expenses or report income.

Staying informed can be as simple as subscribing to IRS newsletters, setting up alerts for major tax news, or working closely with a tax professional who can notify you of changes. Attending webinars and participating in online tax communities can also help business owners stay current.

Here are a few useful IRS newsletters and resources to help:

1. **IRS Tax Tips:** This is a free email newsletter providing easy-to-understand tax tips for small businesses, individuals, and self-employed taxpayers. It's a great way to receive daily updates on important tax matters and changes.

2. **e-News for Small Businesses:** This IRS newsletter focuses specifically on tax issues related to small businesses. It includes information on tax law changes, updates on IRS regulations, and upcoming filing deadlines relevant to small business owners.

3. **IRS Quick Alerts:** Quick Alerts provides notifications regarding IRS e-file changes, system updates, and general e-filing information.

4. **IRS Newswire:** This is a service designed to distribute news releases, fact sheets, and tax-related announcements directly to subscribers. It keeps business owners and tax professionals informed of major news, including changes to tax codes and regulations.

Projected Changes in Federal Tax Policy

Federal tax policy is often shaped by legislative changes, election cycles, and economic conditions, all of which can impact small businesses. As Congress debates new tax legislation, small business owners should be aware of any changes – such as corporate tax rates, capital gains taxes, and deductions for small businesses.

In addition, changes in the economy such as inflation or recessionary concerns, can push lawmakers to enact tax relief measures or alter tax rates to stimulate growth. As political rhetoric intensifies, particularly during election cycles, potential tax reforms may be introduced, meaning small business owners should stay updated about upcoming legislation that could directly impact their tax liabilities.

The Impact of Global Trends on U.S. Small Business Taxes

Global economic trends, such as supply chain disruptions, trade agreements, and international tax regulations, increasingly influence U.S. tax policies. For small businesses, industries like technology, manufacturing, and retail are particularly vulnerable to these changes due to their reliance on global markets and foreign imports. International tax agreements and tariffs may affect how these businesses handle costs, taxes, and compliance with both domestic and foreign regulations.

Additionally, global efforts to implement minimum corporate tax rates, driven by international organizations like the OECD, could eventually impact U.S. tax laws, especially for businesses that engage in cross-border trade. Small businesses that source goods internationally or export products may experience changes in their tax liability depending on how these global agreements are incorporated into U.S. tax policies.

Proactively Preparing for Tax Law Changes

As a small business, you can try to anticipate potential changes in tax laws. By staying engaged with industry-specific groups or associations, business owners can position themselves to preemptively adapt before any changes come into effect.

Legislative updates, often spearheaded by these groups, offer foresight into how new tax policies may impact various industries.

For example, organizations like the National Federation of Independent Business (NFIB) or National Small Business Association (NSBA) work closely with legislators to influence tax law on behalf of small business owners. Through these associations, businesses can stay informed about legislative sessions and impending changes, such as potential adjustments to corporate tax rates, depreciation rules, or job creation credits.

To stay ahead of the game, work with professional tax advisors who closely monitor legislative developments. Tax law professionals stay informed of changes in federal tax and industry-specific regulations. For instance, changes to the Research and Development (R&D) Tax Credit or sector-specific deductions can offer early tax planning opportunities.

Accessing Tax Forms and Publications

IRS Forms and Publications

Business owners can easily access IRS tax forms through the IRS website, such as Schedule C for sole proprietorships, Form 1120 for corporations, and Form 1120-S for S Corporations. These forms, along with others, can be found at 'irs.gov/forms-instructions.' Additionally, the IRS provides detailed publications, like Publication 334, which covers tax guidelines for small businesses, and Publication 583, which explains tax record-keeping requirements. These publications offer step-by-step instructions on filling out tax forms, claiming deductions, and understanding your tax obligations.

State Tax Forms

State-specific tax forms are equally important for small businesses, as they vary by state and include income tax, sales tax, and payroll tax forms. Each state has its own revenue or tax authority department where business owners can access these forms, often through dedicated online portals. For example, businesses based in New York can visit the New York State Department of Taxation and Finance, while California business owners can access the California Department of Tax and Fee Administration.

Filing requirements differ across states. Some states impose income taxes, while others, like Texas and Florida, don't. Additionally, deadlines for filing sales tax and payroll taxes may not align with federal deadlines, so stay updated and current.

Deciphering Tax Forms

Understanding and accurately completing tax forms is critical for small businesses to avoid errors that could result in penalties or delays. Tax forms like Schedule C, Form 1120, and Form 1099 may be cumbersome, with specific fields requiring careful attention. To simplify the process, small business owners should take advantage of tax preparation software with step-by-step guidance and thoroughly read the instructions provided by the IRS. This reduces the risk of common mistakes like the misclassification of expenses or underreporting income.

Additionally, resources like the IRS website and professional tax services can help clarify confusing sections. When unsure about particular forms or deductions, consulting a tax professional is another wise strategy to ensure accuracy and compliance. Using software tools with built-in error-checking functions further helps small business owners stay on track when filing.

Finding and Keeping Important Tax Documents

You'll want to keep accurate and secure records of essential tax documents for compliance and long-term financial planning. Documents such as filed tax returns, W-2s, and receipts for business expenses should be organized and stored safely, either digitally or in the form of physical files. The IRS recommends that businesses retain tax records for at least three years, though some documents related to depreciation or business purchases may need to be kept for a longer period of time.

Small businesses should consider cloud storage solutions with encrypted security features or secure, fireproof filing systems to safeguard these records. Maintaining a digital backup of important files is also helpful in case of physical damage or loss. Having a well-organized record system ensures that tax documents are easily accessible during an audit or when they are needed for future filings.

Understanding Common Tax Forms Through Practical Examples

Below are three practical examples for understanding some common tax forms:

1. **Schedule C (Form 1040):** Used by sole proprietors to report profit or loss from business activities, Schedule C requires the documentation of income and expenses. For instance, a freelance graphic designer would use this form to deduct expenses like software subscriptions and marketing costs. Make sure to keep detailed records of your receipts and other documentation for accuracy.

2. **Form 940 (Federal Unemployment Tax - FUTA):** Businesses with employees must file Form 940 to report unemployment taxes. A common error occurs when businesses confuse state unemployment tax obligations with FUTA. To avoid penalties, businesses must ensure they are filing both federal and state unemployment taxes correctly.

3. **From 1099-MISC:** Independent contractors require businesses to issue a 1099-MISC if payments exceed $600 in a year. Misclassifying employees as contractors could result in back taxes and penalties, so make sure you understand the difference between employees and contractors when issuing this form.

Top eLearning Platforms for Small Business Taxes

Great Webinars for Tax Education

Webinars provide an accessible way for small business owners to stay informed about the latest tax laws and filing requirements. The IRS and the Small Business Administration (SBA) regularly host free webinars that cover essential topics like recent tax legislation, new forms, and common filing errors. Additionally, organizations like the National Federation of Independent Business (NFIB) and private firms offer paid webinars focused on more specialized tax planning strategies for small businesses.

Recommended webinars include the IRS Nationwide Tax Forums, which offer in-depth analysis of tax law changes, and SBA's "Tax Basics for Small Businesses" for newcomers. These webinars allow business owners to learn from tax professionals and ask questions specific to their business's needs.

Joining Small Business Associations

Becoming a member of small business associations, such as the National Federation of Independent Business (NFIB) or the Small Business Administration (SBA), can entitle you to numerous benefits, especially related tax guidance. These associations frequently provide members with up-to-date tax information through exclusive newsletters, webinars, and expert consultations. In addition to educational resources, members gain access to networking events and peer discussions to exchange insights and tax strategies with other business owners. Associations like NFIB even advocate for tax policies favorable to small businesses, keeping members informed about potential tax law changes.

Using Social Media for Community Input and Business Growth

Social media platforms, particularly LinkedIn and Facebook, have become great tools for small business owners seeking tax advice and community support. Joining business-oriented groups or pages dedicated to tax tips and small business strategies allows owners to engage in discussions, ask questions, and receive guidance from peers and experts alike. Platforms like Twitter can also provide real-time tax updates from influencers and tax professionals.

LinkedIn groups like "Small Business Network" and Facebook communities such as "Small Business Tax and Finance" offer a wealth of information, including tax-saving tips, legislative updates, and recommendations for accountants. Following tax influencers, such as @IRSnews or small business tax professionals on social media, can help get you timely advice on filing deadlines, changes in tax laws, and new deductions or credits available.

Maximizing Value from Small Business Associations

Small business associations provide more than just networking opportunities—they offer resources that can directly benefit members' financial health, including mentorship programs, legal support, and specialized tax education. Organizations mentioned above, like the National Small Business Association (NSBA) or the National Federation of Independent Business (NFIB), offer small business owners a wealth of resources designed to address the unique challenges that come with business growth and tax compliance. Membership in these organizations grants access to exclusive educational materials, such as tax seminars, often designed for small businesses. These sessions cover key topics such as managing quarterly tax payments, maximizing deductions, and understanding new regulations. The NFIB, for example, regularly hosts webinars on tax updates and compliance issues, providing members with the tools needed to navigate complex tax situations.

Moreover, members benefit from legal advice, often at discounted rates. This allows them to resolve tax disputes or understand changes in tax law without the full cost of hiring a tax attorney. These associations also advocate on behalf of their members, often lobbying for tax policies that favor small businesses and securing discounts on services like payroll software or tax preparation.

Key Takeaways

- **Constant Vigilance:** Staying updated on the ever-evolving tax code is crucial to remain compliant and maximize savings.

- **Tax Law Changes:** Yearly tax updates can significantly impact your business; knowing what's coming can help you plan ahead.

- **Access to Resources:** IRS forms and publications are readily available online but knowing where and how to use them is key.

- **Educational Tools:** Use eLearning platforms, webinars, and social media networks to stay educated and well-informed.

- **Global Impact:** Tax laws don't just change domestically; international economic trends can also affect U.S. tax policies, especially in the case of certain industries.

- **Organized Document Management:** Keeping tax documents organized ensures quick access and security when needed for audits or future filings.

CHAPTER 10

Beyond Taxes: Basic Bookkeeping and Accounting

"Good order is the foundation of all things."
— Edmund Burke, British statesman and philosopher

Why Bookkeeping Matters for Your Small Business

Small Transactions, Big Impact

At first glance, small transactions—like a $10 office supply purchase or a $15 lunch with a client—might not seem like they would make a difference to your bottom line. But in small business, even the smallest expenses can add up and impact cash flow and profitability. If these transactions aren't properly recorded, you can lose track of them, leading to an inaccurate picture of your financial status.

For example, consider a business with dozens of small daily purchases for supplies, equipment, or travel. Without a structured system for recording these expenses, seeing where money is leaking from your business becomes difficult. Over time, those small, untracked expenses could amount to hundreds or even thousands of dollars, affecting profitability and tax reporting.

Properly tracking small transactions means your books reflect the real financial position of your business. It also allows you to claim all possible deductions when it comes time to file taxes, maximizing your tax savings. More importantly, having a complete record of every expense—no matter how minor—provides transparency and control over your finances, helping you avoid nasty surprises at the month's or quarter's end.

Tracking every dollar spent is a key reason why diligent bookkeeping is a must for small business owners.

Accurate Records: Accuracy is Important

Keeping your financial records accurate leads to the smooth operation of any small business. Organized bookkeeping means you have the necessary data to manage your business effectively, from staying compliant with tax regulations to making informed financial decisions. When tax season rolls around, the ability to provide detailed and accurate records can be the difference between a stress-free filing and a chaotic scramble to gather information. More importantly, maintaining accurate records minimizes errors that could mean penalties, audits, or missed opportunities for valuable deductions.

Inaccurate or incomplete bookkeeping may result in missed expenses that could have reduced your taxable income, costing your business more than necessary. Organized records help with day-to-day management and provide a clear financial picture, making it easier to qualify for loans, plan for expansion, and budget for future expenses. Small business owners can avoid costly mistakes and position their businesses for long-term financial health by keeping thorough, up-to-date records.

Stability Through Regular Financial Check-ups

By scheduling monthly or quarterly financial check-ups, you can assess your business and make proactive decisions before small issues snowball into bigger problems. These check-ups allow you to spot revenue and expense trends, identify growth opportunities, and address potential cash flow issues before they affect your operations.

Without regular reviews, you may miss signs of financial trouble, such as increasing expenses or declining profit margins. Consistent monitoring ensures that you stay in control, allowing you to make adjustments, such as cutting unnecessary expenses or investing in new opportunities.

Avoiding Cash Flow Icebergs

Cash flow is the lifeblood of any small business, and poor bookkeeping can lead to unseen financial pitfalls, or "cash flow icebergs," that threaten to sink your business. These icebergs can include missed payments, unexpected expenses, or unanticipated tax liabilities that arise when your financial records aren't accurately maintained.

By maintaining accurate and up-to-date financial records, you can proactively identify and address potential cash flow challenges before they escalate. Consistent bookkeeping allows you to spot patterns in your cash flow, such as seasonal slowdowns or upcoming financial obligations like payroll or inventory costs. Having this foresight enables you to prepare for these expenses ahead of time, ensuring your business stays financially stable and avoids any unexpected shortfalls. With a clear understanding of your financial situation, you can take the necessary steps to keep your cash flow steady and avoid sudden disruptions.

Accounting Basics For Every Small Business Owner

The ABCs of Debits and Credits

Debits and credits form the core of any bookkeeping or accounting framework. In double-entry bookkeeping, every transaction is recorded in two accounts—one as a debit and the other as a credit. Debits increase asset and expense accounts while decreasing liabilities, equity, and revenue. On the other hand, credits reduce assets and expenses but increase liabilities, equity, and revenue. This system ensures that the books remain balanced by keeping both sides of the equation equal.

Here are a few examples:

1. **Purchasing Office Supplies (Expense & Cash)**
   - **Debit**: Office Supplies (Expense) – Increases the expense account.
   - **Credit**: Cash – Decreases the cash account as you spent money on the supplies.
2. **Taking Out a Loan (Cash & Liability)**
   - **Debit**: Cash – Increases the cash account because you received money from the loan.
   - **Credit**: Loan Payable (Liability) – Increases the liability because you now owe the loan.
3. **Receiving Payment from a Client (Revenue & Accounts Receivable)**
   - **Debit**: Accounts Receivable – Decreases the amount owed to you since the client has paid.
   - **Credit**: Sales Revenue – Increases your revenue for the income received.
4. **Paying Employee Wages (Expense & Cash)**
   - **Debit**: Wages Expense – Increases the wage expense for the business.
   - **Credit**: Cash – Decreases the cash account as you paid out wages.

Understanding debits and credits is needed to keep your books balanced, as every transaction must have equal debits and credits. This means that your financial records are accurate and that your books reflect the true financial position of your business.

Essential Financial Statements: Balance Sheet, Income Statement, and Cash Flow

A solid understanding of your business's core financial statements is necessary for accurate reporting and informed decision-making. These statements provide different insights into the finances and performance of your business.

1. **Balance Sheet:** A balance sheet provides a snapshot of your business's financial position at a particular point in time. It details your assets (what your business owns), liabilities (what your business owes), and equity (the owner's stake in the company). Reviewing this statement regularly helps you evaluate your business's liquidity and financial stability, giving you a clear view of your solvency.
   a. **Assets** include everything your business owns—such as cash, accounts receivable (money owed by customers), inventory, and equipment.
   b. **Liabilities** represent your business's obligations, such as loans, accounts payable (bills you owe), and taxes due.
   c. **Equity** is the owner's stake in the business, which is calculated as Assets minus Liabilities.

Example: If you own a small bakery, your balance sheet might show:

Assets: $10,000 in cash, $5,000 in equipment (ovens, mixers), and $2,000 in inventory (flour, sugar).

Liabilities: A $5,000 loan for kitchen renovations and $1,000 in accounts payable (unpaid ingredient invoices).

Equity: $11,000, which is the difference between your assets and liabilities.

To get started, you would list all of the things your business owns (assets) and owes (liabilities) and then subtract your liabilities from assets to calculate your equity.

2. **Income Statement**: Also called the profit and loss (P&L) statement, this report summarizes your business's revenue, costs, and profits over a set period, such as monthly or annually. It shows how efficiently your business generates income and manages expenses, helping you understand overall profitability and cost management.
   a. **Revenue** is the income your business earns from selling goods or services.
   b. **Expenses** include operating costs such as rent, utilities, wages, and supplies.
   c. **Net Profit/Loss** is calculated by subtracting total expenses from total revenue.

Example: For a freelance graphic designer:

Revenue: You earned $5,000 in design work this month.

Expenses: You spent $500 on software subscriptions, $200 on marketing, and $1,000 on rent for your workspace.

Net Profit: $5,000 (revenue) - $1,700 (expenses) = $3,300 profit for the month.

If you want to get your income statement together, you should track all income sources for your business during a set period, list all operating expenses, including both fixed (rent, utilities) and variable (supplies, advertising) costs. Then, subtract your total expenses from revenue to see if you have a profit or loss.

3. **Cash Flow Statement**: This statement monitors the flow of cash entering and leaving your business, detailing activities related to operations, investments, and financing. This differs

from the income statement, which reflects profits on paper, as the cash flow statement reveals the actual cash your business has on hand to cover expenses and obligations.

a. **Operating Activities**: Cash generated from day-to-day business operations, like sales revenue or paying bills.

b. **Investing Activities**: Cash used for purchasing or selling assets, such as equipment or property.

c. **Financing Activities**: Cash related to borrowing or repaying loans, or transactions with owners, such as issuing equity or paying dividends.

Example: For a retail store:

Operating Activities: You received $20,000 in sales but paid $8,000 in rent and wages.

Investing Activities: You purchased new shelving for $1,500.

Financing Activities: You made a $1,000 loan repayment.

Your cash flow statement would show:

- Net cash from operating activities: $12,000 ($20,000 - $8,000)
- Net cash used in investing activities: -$1,500
- Net cash used in financing activities: -$1,000

To get started with your cash flow statement, track all your cash receipts (sales, loans) and cash payments (bills, loan payments) for the period, and separate them into operating, investing, and financing activities.

Together, these financial reports give you a complete view of your business's financial condition, empowering you to make sound, data-driven decisions.

Double-Entry Bookkeeping

Double-entry bookkeeping forms the foundation of contemporary accounting methods. In this system, every financial transaction is entered into at least two accounts, ensuring that the total amount debited always matches the total amount credited. This approach helps maintain accurate and balanced financial records.

By requiring balanced entries, double-entry bookkeeping reduces the risk of errors and ensures that your books stay aligned, offering a reliable way to track your financial position. This system is built on the principle that for every action, there is an equal and opposite reaction, which in accounting terms means that if one account is debited, another must be credited.

For instance, when a business records a sale, you credit the revenue account while either the cash or accounts receivable account is debited. This process ensures that both sides of the transaction are accounted for, keeping the ledger balanced. In this way, the total assets will always match the combined value of liabilities and equity, maintaining accuracy and reducing the likelihood of bookkeeping errors.

Double-entry bookkeeping is how you get more reliable financial reporting, and it is how you generate key financial statements such as the balance sheet and income statement.

Understanding Assets, Liabilities, and Equity

First grasp the concepts of assets, liabilities, and equity to understand your business's finances.

- **Assets** are everything the business owns, like cash, equipment, inventory, or property.

- **Liabilities** are what the business owes—debts or obligations such as loans, accounts payable, or unpaid taxes. These represent claims against the business's assets.

- **Equity** is what the owner's stake in the company is, which is the difference between total assets and total liabilities. It reflects the residual value left after all liabilities are paid.

The relationship between these forms the accounting equation: Assets = Liabilities + Equity. This equation must always balance. A healthy balance of assets, liabilities, and equity indicates that your business is financially stable.

Decoding Profit and Loss Statements

This statement helps you assess whether your business is operating at a profit or experiencing a loss during a specific period.

The P&L statement has two primary sections. The **revenue** section lists all income earned from sales or services, while the **expenses** section details operating expenses, wages, and utilities. The difference between total revenue and total expenses results in **net profit** (if positive) or **net loss** (if negative).

Business owners use P&L statements to assess financial performance and make decisions about cost control, pricing, and future investments.

Understanding Key Accounting Principles

Accounting principles provide a base for recording, reporting, and interpreting a business's financial information. Here are some of the most widely recognized principles that guide good accounting practices:

1. **Accrual Principle**

Transactions are recorded when they occur, not when cash is received or paid. This means financial statements reflect the true economic activities of the business, providing a more accurate picture.

2. **Consistency Principle**

Once an accounting method is adopted, it should be consistently applied across reporting periods to allow for comparability. If any change in methods occurs, it must be disclosed to maintain transparency and comparability of financial data over time.

3. **Conservatism Principle**

Accountants should record expenses and liabilities as soon as possible, but only recognize revenues when they are sure of being received. This conservative approach prevents overstatement of a company's financial position and promotes cautious reporting.

4. **Going Concern Principle**

Assumes the business will continue to operate into the foreseeable future, which allows financial statements to be prepared without concern for liquidation values. Assets are valued based on their original cost, and the business is treated as an ongoing entity.

5. **Matching Principle**

Expenses must be recognized in the same period as the revenues they help to generate. This means that financial statements are reflective of the company during a specific time frame.

6. **Full Disclosure Principle**

Any information that might affect users' understanding of financial statements must be fully disclosed. This could include footnotes or supplementary schedules explaining significant accounting policies, pending lawsuits, or any other material facts relevant to stakeholders.

7. Materiality Principle

This principle allows accountants to ignore minor errors or omissions if they are not significant enough to affect the decision-making process. Only information deemed material, or that could influence stakeholders, needs to be included in financial reports.

8. Revenue Recognition Principle

Revenue should be recognized when it is earned, not when cash is received. This principle means that revenue is recorded in the period in which the sale occurs or service is performed, aligning with the accrual accounting method.

9. Objectivity Principle

All financial statements and transactions must be based on objective, verifiable evidence. This means that records such as receipts, invoices, and bank statements must back up financial reporting, ensuring accuracy and preventing manipulation.

10. Cost Principle

Assets are recorded at their original purchase cost, not at their current market value. This principle provides consistency in reporting and prevents businesses from arbitrarily inflating asset values in financial statements.

11. Time Period Principle

This principle states that businesses should report their financial performance in specific, consistent time periods, such as monthly, quarterly, or annually.

How to Set Up a Chart of Accounts

A chart of accounts (COA) is an organizational tool for businesses, providing a structured way to categorize all financial transactions. Whether you run a small business or a large corporation, setting up an accurate COA can help you maintain proper financial records. Here's how you can establish an effective COA:

1. **Understand the Business Structure**

   Before setting up a COA, you need to understand the nature of your business. The COA should be made to fit your specific operations, industry, and reporting requirements. For instance, a retail company may need more categories for inventory, while a service-based business may focus on labor-related expenses.

2. **Define Major Account Categories**

   At the top level, a COA is divided into several primary categories. These typically include:
   - **Assets**
   - **Liabilities**
   - **Equity**
   - **Revenue**
   - **Expenses**

Each category can then be broken down into subcategories for better tracking and detail.

3. **Assign Account Numbers**

   Each account within the COA should be assigned a unique number, which makes it easier to record and track transactions. For example, asset accounts may start with 1000, liabilities with 2000, and so on. This numbering system should follow a logical order and be flexible enough to allow for future expansion.

4. **Balance Simplicity and Detail**

   While the COA should provide enough detail to track financial activities accurately, it should not be overly complex. Aim for simplicity by including only accounts that are relevant to the business, while ensuring that there is enough detail to generate useful financial reports.

5. **Review and Update Regularly**

As your business grows, your COA should evolve. Regularly reviewing and updating the accounts will ensure that the chart remains relevant and reflects the current operations of the business.

Tools to Simplify Your Bookkeeping and Accounting

Exploring Accounting Software Options

Choosing the right accounting software can make managing your business's finances significantly easier. Popular options like **QuickBooks**, **FreshBooks**, and **Xero** are designed to automate many bookkeeping tasks, streamline data entry, and provide easy access to financial information.

QuickBooks

QuickBooks is one of the most widely used accounting software platforms, particularly for small to medium-sized businesses. It offers a set of tools that cover nearly every aspect of accounting, from invoicing to payroll to tax preparation.

Pros:

- **Full-Featured**: QuickBooks provides a wide range of features including invoicing, expense tracking, inventory management, payroll, and tax preparation. This makes it an all-in-one solution for businesses that need extensive accounting capabilities.

- **Scalable**: It's suitable for small startups as well as larger businesses. QuickBooks offers different versions, such as QuickBooks Self-Employed for freelancers and QuickBooks Online for more complicated businesses.

- **Strong Reporting Tools**: The software generates detailed financial reports like profit and loss statements, balance sheets, and cash flow statements..

- **Integrations**: QuickBooks integrates with various business apps such as PayPal, Square, and Shopify, making it easier to sync data from different platforms.

- **Payroll**: Offers seamless payroll processing, including automatic tax calculations and direct deposit.

Cons:

- **Cost**: QuickBooks can be expensive, especially for businesses that need advanced features. The monthly subscription can add up, and additional costs for payroll and advanced reporting are often needed.

- **Learning Curve**: Due to its extensive features, QuickBooks can be a bit complicated for beginners. It requires some time to fully understand and use all its tools effectively.

- **Customer Support**: Some users report slow or unhelpful customer support experiences, particularly during tax season when help is most needed.

Best for:

Businesses of any size that need an all-in-one accounting solution with advanced reporting and tax preparation features. It's ideal for small to medium-sized businesses that want to scale or require payroll capabilities.

FreshBooks

FreshBooks is designed with small businesses and freelancers in mind, particularly those in service-based industries. It offers a simple, user-friendly interface and focuses heavily on invoicing and time-tracking features.

Pros:

- **User-Friendly**: FreshBooks is incredibly easy to use, making it ideal for business owners with little to no accounting experience. The interface is intuitive, allowing users to quickly generate invoices, track time, and manage expenses.

- **Invoicing and Time-Tracking**: FreshBooks excels in invoicing, allowing you to create, send, and follow up on invoices easily. It also provides time-tracking features, making it a great choice for service-based businesses that need to bill clients for hours worked.

- **Affordability**: FreshBooks offers competitive pricing, with plans designed for businesses with simpler accounting needs. It's often cheaper than QuickBooks.

- **Mobile App**: The mobile app is well-designed and allows users to manage their accounts, send invoices, and track expenses on the go.

- **Customer Support**: FreshBooks is known for its responsive and helpful customer support, which can be a lifesaver for small business owners who need quick answers.

Cons:

- **Limited Features**: While FreshBooks is excellent for invoicing and time-tracking, it lacks some of the advanced accounting features found in QuickBooks, such as in depth payroll or inventory management tools.

- **Not Ideal for Larger Businesses**: FreshBooks is best suited for freelancers and small businesses. It doesn't scale as well for businesses with complex accounting needs or a larger number of employees.

Best for:

Freelancers and small service-based businesses that need easy invoicing, time-tracking, and basic accounting features.

Xero

Xero is a cloud-based accounting platform that's known for its flexibility and integrations. It's especially useful for businesses that want the ability to collaborate with accountants or other team members remotely.

Pros:

- **Cloud-Based Collaboration**: Xero's cloud-based platform allows multiple users, including accountants and business owners, to access the system from anywhere. This makes it a great tool for teams that need to collaborate remotely.

- **Integrations**: Xero integrates with over 800 business apps, including CRM tools, inventory management platforms, and payment processors. This makes it one of the most flexible accounting platforms for businesses that need specialized tools.

- **Real-Time Dashboards**: The software provides real-time dashboards that show a clear view of your financial data, including bank balances, invoices, and expenses. This allows for better decision-making with up-to-date financial information.

- **Affordable Pricing**: Xero is competitively priced compared to QuickBooks, with tiered pricing plans that accommodate different business needs.

- **Unlimited Users**: Unlike QuickBooks, Xero allows unlimited users at no additional cost, which is beneficial for growing businesses that need multiple people accessing the software.

Cons:

- **Limited Payroll**: Xero has fewer payroll options compared to QuickBooks, and its payroll feature is only available in select countries. Businesses that need payroll services may need to integrate third-party software.

- **Learning Curve**: While Xero is easier than QuickBooks, it still requires some learning, especially for users unfamiliar with accounting software.

- **Customer Support**: Xero relies heavily on email support, which can be slow.

Best for:

Small to medium-sized businesses looking for a cloud-based solution that offers flexibility, collaboration, and strong integration options. Xero is ideal for businesses that need to manage financials remotely or rely on third-party apps for specialized tasks.

Which Software is Best for You?

- **Choose QuickBooks** if you need a comprehensive accounting solution with strong reporting tools, payroll capabilities, and scalability for future growth.

- **Choose FreshBooks** if you are a freelancer or run a small service-based business and prioritize ease of use, invoicing, and time tracking.

- **Choose Xero** if you value cloud-based collaboration, need integration with multiple business tools, and want a flexible solution for remote teamwork.

Essential Bookkeeping Tools

In addition to accounting software, a few essential bookkeeping tools can further streamline your business's financial management:

- **Expense Trackers** like Expensify or Shoeboxed make it easy to track and categorize business expenses.
- **Receipt Management Apps** such as Receipt Bank help you store and organize receipts digitally, ensuring you have a record for tax time.
- **Invoicing Systems** like Bill.com simplify the process of sending, receiving, and managing payments, helping you stay on top of cash flow.

These tools complement accounting software by keeping financial records organized and easily accessible.

Cloud-Based Solutions

Cloud-based bookkeeping tools have revolutionized how small businesses handle their financial management. Platforms like **QuickBooks Online, Xero, and FreshBooks** offer real-time access to financial information from any device, making them particularly beneficial for businesses with remote teams or multiple locations.

A key benefit of using cloud-based tools is **enhanced data security**. These systems store your financial information on secure, remote servers, minimizing the chances of data loss due to equipment failures or other technical issues. This safeguards your data and also ensures it's easily accessible when needed. Cloud tools also enable automatic updates, ensuring your software remains up-to-date without manual intervention.

Another key benefit is **collaboration**. Cloud-based tools allow multiple users to access and work on financial records simultaneously, making it easier for accountants, bookkeepers, and business owners to collaborate in real-time.

Evolving Your Tools to Stay Ahead

Your financial management needs will grow as your business does. It's important to regularly evaluate and update your bookkeeping and accounting tools to keep pace with changes in technology and business demands. Emerging tools offer automation, artificial intelligence, and integration with other business systems, helping you manage finances more efficiently.

By staying current with the latest tools, you can optimize your bookkeeping process, minimize errors, and ensure that your business's financial records remain organized and up to date.

Checklists: Essential Bookkeeping and Accounting Tasks

Monthly Financial Tasks

Staying on top of monthly bookkeeping tasks is essential for maintaining your business's finances. Key tasks include:

- **Reconciling Bank Accounts**: Match your bank statements with your accounting records to ensure that all transactions are recorded properly and accurately. This helps identify discrepancies, such as missed transactions or bank fees.
- **Categorizing Expenses**: Regularly categorize your business expenses to organize your financial data. Properly labeled expenses will make it easier to track spending and maximize deductions during tax season.
- **Reviewing Cash Flow**: Take time each month to review your cash flow—money coming in versus money going out. This allows you to spot potential cash shortages and make

adjustments, such as deferring expenses or accelerating collections, to maintain a positive cash flow.

- **Invoicing and Payments**: Stay on top of invoicing clients and follow up on unpaid invoices to ensure timely payment.

Consistent monthly reviews will keep your finances organized and reduce stress at tax time.

Quarterly Review Must-dos

Quarterly financial reviews are an opportunity to assess the bigger picture and make strategic adjustments. Some of the more important quarterly tasks include:

- **Financial Health Review**: Examine your income statements, balance sheets, and cash flow statements to assess overall financial performance. Look for trends or discrepancies that may require attention.

- **Tax Estimations**: Calculate your estimated taxes and make tax payments to avoid penalties.

- **Budget Adjustments**: Compare your actual performance against your budget and adjust it for the upcoming quarter. If you're overspending in certain areas, identify ways to cut costs or reallocate resources.

Year-End Accounting Chores

Year-end accounting chores are crucial for wrapping up your financial year and preparing for tax filing. Key tasks include:

- **Preparing Financial Statements**: Generate year-end financial statements, including the income statement, balance sheet, and cash flow statement.

- **Reviewing Expenses**: Review and categorize all business expenses to ensure you've claimed all possible deductions.

- **Organizing Tax Documents**: Gather and organize all necessary tax documents, such as W-2s, 1099s, and receipts, to simplify the tax filing process.

Completing these tasks ensures a smooth transition into the new financial year and helps you stay compliant with tax regulations.

Planning for Tax Season

Planning for tax season will help avoid last-minute stress. Key steps include:

- **Gathering Receipts**: Collect and organize receipts for all business-related expenses to ensure accurate deductions.

- **Updating Records**: Review and update your bookkeeping records to ensure they are complete and accurate for tax filing.

- **Reviewing Tax Deductions and Credits**: Note which deductions and credits you can use to reduce your tax liability. Consult with a tax professional if necessary to maximize your savings.

Proactive tax planning ensures a smoother filing process and fewer surprises.

Advanced Topics in Bookkeeping and Accounting

Depreciation and Amortization Methods

Depreciation and **amortization** are fundamental concepts for accounting, particularly when dealing with long-term assets. Both allow businesses to allocate the cost of an asset over its useful life, using one of these methods:

- **Straight-Line Depreciation**: This is the simplest and most common method, where the cost of an asset is evenly distributed over its useful life. For example, if you purchase machinery for $10,000 with a useful life of 10 years, you would depreciate it by $1,000 per year.

- **Declining Balance Depreciation**: This method accelerates depreciation, meaning you write off more of the asset's cost in the early years of its life. For instance, a business might use a double-declining balance, where depreciation is calculated as a percentage of the asset's remaining value each year.

- **Units of Production Depreciation**: This method allocates depreciation based on actual usage, suitable for assets like machinery or vehicles that wear out over time. If a machine is expected to produce 100,000 units over its life and produces 10,000 units in the first year, then 10% of its value is depreciated in that year.

Similarly, **amortization** applies to intangible assets such as patents or trademarks. It operates like depreciation but is used for non-physical assets.

Accounting for Bad Debts and Write-Offs

Not all customers will pay their bills, and it's important to account for this. When a business anticipates that some of its receivables may never be collected, it must record **bad debts** using one of these methods:

- **Allowance Method**: This method estimates bad debts in advance, so that accounts receivable on the balance sheet are not overstated. For instance, if you estimate that 5% of receivables will be uncollectible, you create an allowance for bad debts and expense that amount immediately.

- **Direct Write-Off Method**: Here, bad debts are only accounted for when they are confirmed to be uncollectible. The company writes off the amount directly from accounts receivable and records it as an expense.

Understanding Financial Ratios and Metrics for Business Analysis

Financial ratios are tools for analyzing business performance, offering insights into profitability, liquidity, efficiency, and solvency. There are countless ratios you can use, but here are a few of the more common types:

- **Profitability Ratios**: Metrics such as **Gross Profit Margin** and **Net Profit Margin** help assess how effectively a company is generating profit relative to sales.

- **Liquidity Ratios**: Ratios like the **Current Ratio** (current assets divided by current liabilities) evaluate a company's ability to meet short-term obligations.

- **Efficiency Ratios**: Metrics like **Inventory Turnover** (cost of goods sold divided by average inventory) show how efficiently a business manages its assets.

- **Solvency Ratios**: The **Debt-to-Equity Ratio** helps assess a company's long-term financial stability, indicating how much debt is used to finance assets compared to equity.

Internal Controls in Bookkeeping and Accounting

Establishing Internal Controls to Prevent Fraud and Errors

Internal controls are mechanisms implemented within an organization to ensure the accuracy and reliability of financial reporting, safeguard assets, and promote operational efficiency. Effective internal controls can help prevent fraud and minimize errors.

Segregation of Duties, Authorization of Transactions, and Regular Audits

One of the most fundamental principles of internal controls is the **segregation of duties**. This involves dividing responsibilities among different employees so that no single person controls all aspects of a financial transaction.

- **Segregation of Duties**: For example, the person who processes payments should not be the same person who reconciles the bank account. This reduces the risk of fraud and errors.

- **Authorization of Transactions**: Requiring management approval for large transactions ensures that expenditures align with business goals and prevents unauthorized spending.

- **Regular Audits**: Regular internal audits, whether conducted by an internal audit team or an external firm, can identify discrepancies, ensure compliance with regulations, and improving financial reporting accuracy.

Using Technology and Software to Enhance Internal Controls

Advancements in accounting software have made it easier to implement and enforce internal controls. **Cloud-based accounting software** like QuickBooks and Xero allows businesses to set user permissions, so only authorized individuals can access sensitive financial information. These platforms also provide audit trails, which help track who accessed or modified certain financial data.

For example, **AI-driven tools** can automatically flag unusual transactions or inconsistencies in records, reducing the risk of fraud. These tools are increasingly important as businesses scale and transactions become more complex.

Ethical Considerations in Accounting & Bookkeeping

Importance of Ethics in Accounting

Accounting ethics help maintain the trust of stakeholders, including clients, investors, employees, and the public. An accountant or bookkeeper is expected to adhere to high ethical standards, for accuracy, transparency, and honesty in financial reporting.

Common Ethical Dilemmas and How to Handle Them

Common ethical dilemmas include pressure to falsify financial records, underreporting income, or overstating expenses to reduce tax liabilities. If an accountant is asked to engage in these activities, the best course of action is to refuse, report the issue to a higher authority, or, if necessary, resign.

Professional Standards and Codes of Conduct for Bookkeepers and Accountants

Professional organizations such as the **American Institute of Certified Public Accountants (AICPA)** have established codes of conduct that accountants and bookkeepers must follow. These standards emphasize the importance of integrity, objectivity, confidentiality, and due care.

Case Studies and Practical Examples

Real-World Examples of Common Bookkeeping Scenarios

Case Study 1: A Small Retail Business Improving Inventory Records

A small boutique retail store found itself struggling with inventory management. The owner relied on manual tracking methods, often leading to discrepancies in their inventory records. When performing balance sheet reconciliations, they frequently noticed that the recorded inventory didn't match the physical stock. This mismanagement affected their financial statements, leading to inaccurate financial reports and difficulties in managing cash flow.

To resolve this, the business implemented inventory tracking software that integrated directly with their accounting system. This software automated the process of tracking inventory in real-time, updating their system whenever sales were made or new stock was ordered. They also began conducting monthly inventory reconciliations for accuracy. As a result, they were able to keep their balance sheet accurate, forecast their cash flow more effectively, and avoid over-ordering or under-stocking. The system also provided clear visibility into which items were selling well, helping them make decisions about purchasing and promotions.

Case Study 2: A Service-Based Business Automating Invoicing to Improve Cash Flow

A marketing consultancy that billed clients for services after completion frequently faced delays in payments, leading to a cycle of cash flow problems. The business owner manually generated invoices and often forgot to follow up on overdue payments, allowing outstanding invoices to accumulate and their working capital to deplete.

Recognizing the inefficiency, the consultancy switched to an automated invoicing system using FreshBooks, which allowed them to streamline their invoicing process. The system generated and sent invoices as soon as a project was completed and automatically followed up on overdue payments. The platform also allowed clients to pay directly online, making it easier and faster for clients to settle their bills. Within a few months, late payments were reduced by 40%, which significantly improved cash flow stability. Additionally, the time saved on manual invoicing freed up the owner to focus on acquiring new clients and growing the business.

Case Study 3: A Growing eCommerce Company Managing Payroll Across State Lines

A rapidly expanding eCommerce company started hiring employees from multiple states, which brought new challenges in managing payroll and tax compliance. Each state had different tax rates, regulations, and filing requirements, making payroll processing increasingly complex. This complexity led to errors in tax withholding, causing compliance issues and potential penalties.

To address this, the company adopted cloud-based accounting software that included payroll management features. The software automatically calculated payroll taxes based on each employee's location, ensured that all taxes were correctly withheld, and even generated the necessary state-specific tax forms for submission. Additionally, the platform provided clear reporting on payroll expenses and tax liabilities, allowing the company to track costs effectively as they expanded into new markets. By automating payroll and tax filing, the company stayed compliant with state-specific regulations, reduced the risk of penalties, and saved significant time that would have otherwise been spent on manual payroll processing.

Key Takeaways

- **Track Small Transactions**: Even the smallest financial transactions can impact your business's bottom line if left untracked.

- **Accurate Records Matter**: Maintaining organized, accurate financial records helps with compliance, tax filing, and financial planning.

- **Know Your Financial Statements**: Get to understand your balance sheets, income statements, and cash flow statements.

- **Use the Right Tools**: Utilize bookkeeping software and cloud-based solutions to streamline accounting processes and improve accuracy.

- **Monthly and Yearly Check-ups**: Regular financial reviews and year-end preparations help maintain financial stability and prepare for tax season.

- **Stay Organized**: Use checklists to ensure all bookkeeping tasks are completed on time, minimizing errors and avoiding cash flow issues.

FINAL THOUGHTS

Mastering Small Business Taxes and Financial Health

We've gone through small business taxes, bookkeeping, and accounting throughout this book. You've learned how different tax types—income, self-employment, excise, and employment taxes—affect your business and how your choice of business structure directly impacts your tax obligations. You are now better prepared to manage your business's tax responsibilities and ensure compliance with IRS regulations.

However, mastering small business taxes goes beyond understanding tax forms. Precise bookkeeping is essential for running your business. Whether it's tracking minor transactions or generating financial statements, maintaining thorough records ensures that your business's financial data is both updated and accurate.

This helps you claim all available tax deductions and positions your business for growth by providing a clear view of its financial health.

Key Takeaways

- **Understand Your Tax Obligations:** Knowing which taxes apply to your business, such as income tax and self-employment tax, helps you avoid surprises and plan for the future. You can prevent penalties and maintain compliance by staying up to date with tax regulations and deadlines.

- **Accurate Record-Keeping is Crucial:** Whether tracking small transactions, categorizing expenses, or preparing year-end financial statements, accurate bookkeeping is essential for your business's success. Organized records help you identify financial trends, improve cash flow, and maximize tax deductions.

- **Financial Reports Are Essential for Assessing Business Health:** Regularly examining your balance sheet, income statement, and cash flow statement helps provide a clear picture of your company's financial status. These reports deliver valuable insights into areas like profitability, liquidity, and overall performance, helping you make well-informed business decisions.

- **Use Technology to Streamline Accounting:** We've covered tools like QuickBooks, FreshBooks, and Xero, which simplify bookkeeping by automating tasks and providing real-time access to financial data. Cloud-based solutions enable collaboration, help secure your financial information and allow it to be accessible online from wherever you are.

- **Proactive Tax Planning is Essential:** If you wait until tax season to start thinking about your tax obligations, you can easily fall behind. By proactively estimating quarterly taxes, tracking potential deductions throughout the year, and preparing in advance, you can avoid last-minute scrambling and reduce your tax burden.

Looking Ahead: Putting Knowledge into Action

Now that you've absorbed these key concepts, the next step is to put them into practice. Begin by setting up monthly and quarterly financial reviews, ensuring that your records are complete and current. Really understand your financial statements and what they reveal about your business's performance. Start planning for tax season early by gathering receipts, organizing documents, and consulting with a tax professional if necessary.

Beyond taxes, this book has introduced bookkeeping and accounting principles—the backbone of your business's financial management. Whether you're just starting out or looking to refine your processes, these principles will guide you in making better financial decisions, managing your cash flow, and planning for the future.

As your business grows, your financial management practices will evolve. It's important to stay flexible and adjust your bookkeeping and accounting tools to meet evolving requirements. Stay informed about new tax laws, emerging technologies, and best practices to ensure your business remains financially stable.

Final Thoughts

Mastering your business's financial health is an ongoing process. The concepts in this book provide the foundation you need to make well-researched decisions, avoid expensive mistakes, and position your business for long-term success. By staying organized, proactive, and flexible, you can get through the complexities of small business taxes and keep your business financially healthy.

You have the tools and knowledge, so let's take action. Try doing some of what you've learned, and revisit sections of the book as your business grows and evolves. Start with small steps—track your expenses more diligently, review your monthly financial statements, and plan for tax season.

If you found this book helpful, I encourage you to share your opinion by leaving a review on Amazon. Your feedback helps other small business owners discover valuable resources like this one, allowing us to continue providing helpful content. Here's to your success in mastering the financial side of your business—your journey is just beginning!

Glossary And Helpful Resources

Free calculators, forms, and tools beneficial for small business owners

1. **Calculators**

   o TaxCaster by TurboTax: A tool that helps estimate your tax refund.

   o Small Business Tax Calculator by Taxfyle: It provides an estimated tax refund or tax liability for small businesses.

   o Self-Employed Tax Calculator by TaxAct: This calculator offers accurate estimates of tax obligations according to prevailing self-employment tax rates.

   o Business Tax Expense Calculator: For comprehensive self-employed income tax calculation.

   o Self-Employed Tax Calculator & Expense Estimator by TurboTax: Helps find common self-employment tax deductions, write-offs, and business expenses for 1099 filers.

2. **Forms**

   o Free File by IRS: Helps prepare and file your federal income tax return online for free.

   o W-4 Withholding Calculator by TurboTax: An essential tool for assessing how much federal income tax should be withheld from your paycheck.

3. **Other Tools**

   o Tax Tools and Calculators by H&R Block: A range of convenient tax tools, including a personalized tax prep checklist.

- o Free Resources by KeeperTax: Interactive tools and expert-written guides to make taxes easy for freelancers and 1099 contractors.

- o Free Self-Employed Income Tax Preparation by FreeTaxUSA: Offers hundreds of deductions, write-offs, and credits built into the online software.

Glossary

Accrual Accounting: An accounting method where revenue is recorded when earned and expenses are recorded when incurred, irrespective of when cash is exchanged.

Assets: Property or items of value owned by a business.

Balance Sheet: A financial statement that provides a snapshot of what a company owns (assets), owes (liabilities), and the shareholders' investment (equity) at a specific point in time.

Bookkeeping: The process of recording all financial transactions made by a business.

Cash Flow: The total amount of money being transferred in and out of a business, especially affecting liquidity.

Deductions: Expenses that can be subtracted from a company's income before it is subject to taxation.

Depreciation: The gradual reduction in the value of an asset over time due to wear and tear or obsolescence.

Equity: The ownership interest of investors in a business, calculated as assets minus liabilities.

Gross Income: The total income from all sources before taxes and other deductions.

Income Statement: A financial document that shows how much profit or loss a business has made over a period.

Liabilities: The debts and obligations owed by a business.

Net Income: The company's total earnings, also known as net profit. It's calculated as revenues minus expenses, interest, and taxes.

Overhead: The ongoing business expenses not directly tied to creating a product or service.

Payroll Taxes: Taxes an employer withholds and/or pays on behalf of their employees based on the wage or salary of the employee.

Profit & Loss Statement: Also known as an income statement, it provides a detailed look at a company's revenues, costs, expenses, and net income over a period.

Retained Earnings: The portion of net income which is retained by the corporation rather than distributed to its owners as dividends.

Revenue: The income generated from normal business operations and includes discounts and deductions for returned merchandise.

Self-Employment Tax: The tax that a small business owner must pay to the federal government to fund Medicare and Social Security.

Tax Credit: A tax incentive which allows certain taxpayers to subtract the amount of the credit from the total they owe the state.

Tax Deduction: A reduction in tax obligation from a taxpayer's gross taxable income.

Write-offs: Expenses that can be deducted from taxable income to reduce the amount of tax owed.

A Parting Gift

As a way of saying thank you for your purchase, we're giving you our *"7-Figure Business Toolkit"* that includes six FREE downloads that are exclusive to our book readers!

Here's what you'll get:

1. **The Small Biz Tax Deduction Checklist** – An easy checklist for the most common small business tax deductions.

2. **The IRS Audit Survival Guide** – Discover exactly what to do if the IRS comes knocking for an audit of your business.

3. **The Negotiation Mastery Cheat Sheet** – Master the art of negotiation and get a massive edge in your business.

4. **The Start Your LLC Checklist** – This step-by-step PDF shows you exactly how to get your LLC up and running.

5. **The Top 7 Websites To Start Your LLC** – Save hours on research and choose the best website to start your LLC.

6. **The Mindfulness Hacks for Entrepreneurs PDF** – Stay cool, calm, and collected through all the ups and downs of your business journey.

To download your 7-Figure Business Toolkit, you can go to monroemethod.com/taxes **or simply scan the QR code below:**

Can You Do Us a Favor?

Thanks for checking out our book.

We're confident this will help you build your LLC and create a thriving business!

Would you take 60 seconds and write a quick blurb about this book on Amazon?

Reviews are the best way for independent authors (like us) to get noticed, sell more books, and spread our message to as many people as possible. We also read every review and use the feedback to write future revisions – and future books, even.

Thank you – we really appreciate your support.

About the Author

Garrett Monroe is a pen name for a team of writers with business experience in various industries, like coaching, sales, AI, real estate, copywriting, accounting, etc. They've built teams, understand how to manage people, and know what it takes to be a successful entrepreneur. These writers have come together to share their knowledge and produce a series of business books and help you take your business endeavors to the next level.

Printed in Great Britain
by Amazon

56797035R00086